Global Nuclear
Energy Risks

About the Book and Author

Global Nuclear Energy Risks:
The Search for Preventive Medicine
Bennett Ramberg

Almost two dozen nations currently generate nuclear energy, and eighteen more are planning to construct reactors in the near future. This expansion increases the need for the international community to find ways to meet five basic security challenges: national and subnational diversion of nuclear materials for weapons, subnational sabotage of nuclear facilities, wartime destruction, and major accidents. To date, international efforts to address these problems have included the Non-Proliferation Treaty, the Latin American nuclear-free zone, the International Atomic Energy Agency, and the nuclear suppliers conference. Despite these laudable achievements, uneven approaches to obligations and inherent problems in the international agreements may weaken their effectiveness. New approaches must be sought in order to ensure safe, peaceful development of nuclear energy.

Dr. Ramberg explores various methods of enhancing existing practices through the use of "preventive medicine." After outlining the current nuclear regime and examining its weaknesses, he evaluates the desirability and practicality of seven "international nuclear review" options focused on preventing a global nuclear disaster.

Bennett Ramberg is a research associate at the Center for International and Strategic Affairs, University of California, Los Angeles, and co-editor of *Globalism vs. Realism: International Relations' Third Debate* (Westview 1982) and *Nuclear Power Plants as Weapons for the Enemy: An Unrecognized Military Peril* (1984).

To the memories of my dearest friends—
my dad, Isaac Ramberg, and
my uncle, David Lipsky

Written under the auspices of the
Center for International and Strategic Affairs,
University of California, Los Angeles.
A list of other Center publications appears at the end of this book.

Global Nuclear Energy Risks

The Search for Preventive Medicine

Bennett Ramberg

Westview Press / Boulder and London

This book was written under the auspices of the Center for International and Strategic Affairs, University of California, Los Angeles.

Published in 1986 in the United States of America by Westview Press, Inc.; Frederick A. Praeger, Publisher; 5500 Central Avenue, Boulder, Colorado 80301

Library of Congress Cataloging in Publication Data
Ramberg, Bennett.
   Global nuclear energy risks.
   Bibliography: p.
   Includes index.
   1. Nuclear nonproliferation.   2. Nuclear energy—
International cooperation.   3. Nuclear power plants—
Security measures.   I. Title.
JX1974.73.R34   1985   327.1'74   84-22909
ISBN 0-86531-667-8

Printed and bound in the United States of America

10   9   8   7   6   5   4   3   2   1

Contents

Tables

Preface

The nuclear industry today is in serious recession. In the United States a recent government report found that "no nuclear plant now operating or still under active construction has been ordered since 1974, and every year since has seen a decrease in total utility commitment to nuclear power."[1] Abroad, with few exceptions, the nuclear energy industry is sputtering. Whether or not the industry worldwide can revive is a matter of conjecture. Industry and government officials in the United States and elsewhere argue that the inevitable increase of electrical consumption in the years ahead coupled with the retirement of older oil- and coal-fired plants makes a renaissance of nuclear power inevitable. Critics counter that challenges confronting the industry are insuperable. Beyond cost, safety, and an absence of public confidence, they point to strategic problems, namely, the potential link of the nuclear industry to weapons proliferation, terrorism, and radioactive contamination that could result from military destruction of nuclear plants and from major accidents.

If the industry is to prosper in the coming years, it must meet each of these challenges. As two prominent students of the industry, William Walker and Mans Lönnroth, note, "If demand does return, however modestly, reliance on 'muddling through' may place too much faith in the wisdom of peoples and governments."[2] This book addresses the strategic challenges and proposes alternative international remedies set in historical and regulatory contexts that suggest that nations should increase international scrutiny of atomic power in order to minimize risks.

There are five major security risks attached to worldwide growth of nuclear energy: national diversion of nuclear materials for weapons, subnational diversion for weapons, subnational sabotage of nuclear facilities, wartime destruction, and major accidents. Thus far, these risks have been minimized by the Non-Proliferation Treaty (NPT), the International Atomic Energy Agency (IAEA), the European Atomic Energy Community (EUR-ATOM), the Agency for the Prohibition of Nuclear Weapons in Latin America, and by nuclear suppliers' safeguards and guidelines. However, uneven application of obligations and inherent deficiencies in these control measures may decrease their effectiveness in the future, so novel remedies must be sought and applied.

More authoritative nuclear energy control measures offer the kind of preventive medicine[3] that can limit strategic nuclear energy risks. The earlier and the more extensively these measures are applied, the greater will be their effectiveness. The measures fall into two basic categories: primary and secondary prevention. Primary prevention involves averting subnational diversion, sabotage, wartime destruction, and major accidents; secondary prevention entails halting the international proliferation of nuclear weapons.

Proposed here are seven International Nuclear Reviews (INRs), distinguished by their degree of utility in anticipating nuclear problems. The INRs build upon a historical record suggesting that nations are increasingly sensitive to the dangers posed by nuclear energy and are willing to take measures to minimize them. The INRs have grown out of the experience of the Nuclear Regulatory Commission, the Energy Research and Development Administration (ERDA), the Nuclear Non-Proliferation Act of 1978, the U.S. Arms Control and Disarmament Agency (ACDA), EURATOM, the Consultative Committee (Cocom), and the International Bank for Reconstruction and Development (the World Bank), plus the IAEA's physical security guidelines, which attempt to anticipate technological risks, including, in most cases, those derived from atomic power. Proposals of scholars and officials in the industry have also been considered in the development of these INRs.

The rationalization behind the INRs is developed in the five chapters of this book. Chapter 1 explores the strategic problems posed by nuclear energy. Chapter 2 reviews currently applied risk-prevention measures. Chapter 3 establishes an empirical basis for the INR alternatives. Chapter 4 describes the INRs, and Chapter 5 anticipates questions about their viability.

Both opponents and proponents of nuclear energy may feel uncomfortable with the options I offer. Opponents may see them as an effort to sustain a dying industry. If indeed the industry is dying, it is unlikely that my suggestions will revive it. If it is not dying, adoption of my suggestions (or facsimiles thereof) can make nuclear power safer. I advocate greater international regulation in an industry that many feel is over-regulated, but the atomic energy industry cannot withstand many more accidents like that at Three Mile Island, more military bombardment of reactors like the 1981 Israeli attack, or the realization of other strategic threats. Although this study may not satisfy everyone, I hope at the very least that it stimulates new thought on the issues involved.

Bennett Ramberg

Acknowledgments

I am indebted to several reviewers for valuable comments. In the early development of this book Jim Digby of the RAND Corporation afforded me the opportunity to test my conclusions before the California Seminar on International Security and Foreign Policy. Gregory Jones of Pan Heuristics and Patrick O'Heffernan critiqued my initial draft. Randy Rydell of the Lawrence Livermore Laboratory reviewed the pre-publication manuscript. I wish to extend special thanks to Warren Donnelly of the Congressional Research Service for an exceptional line by line assessment. Discussions with Michael Brenner of the University of Pittsburgh and Lillian Katz further sharpened my argument. The UCLA Center for International and Strategic Affairs provided financial support. Above all, my deepest gratitude goes to my parents for their continuing interest in my work.

B.R.

1
The Problem

The Nuclear Market

In late 1983 there were 529 nuclear power reactors in operation, under construction, or on order in thirty-eight countries (see Table 1.1). In several nations nuclear energy already generates a significant amount of electricity. In 1981 the share of electric power generated by nuclear facilities was 38 percent in France, 36 percent in Sweden, 28 percent in Switzerland, 25 percent in Belgium and Taiwan, 16 percent in Japan, 14 percent in Germany, 13 percent in Britain, and 12 percent in the United States.[1] Table 1.2 indicates that electricity generation from atomic power will increase for many nations in the years to come.

Although this growth is impressive, it is clearly not as expansive as anticipated just a few short years ago. In the mid-1970s the International Atomic Energy Agency (IAEA) predicted that nuclear power generation worldwide would reach 1,500 gigawatts (gwe) by the year 1990 and up to 5,000 gwe by 2000.[2] Present predictions are substantially lower. Looking at member countries of the Organization for Economic Cooperation and Development (OECD)—Austria, Belgium, Canada, Denmark, Finland, France, the Federal Republic of Germany, Italy, Japan, Luxembourg, the Netherlands, Portugal, Spain, Sweden, Switzerland, the United Kingdom, and the United States—puts this into clearer focus. Table 1.3 shows that estimates for Western European nuclear power generation by 2000 have been reduced by over 70 percent since 1975—likewise for the United States. Even these forecasts may be optimistic. Expectations were mostly wishful thinking and simplistic linear extrapolations based on the assumption that energy consumption would continue to rise in the future

Table 1.1

Nuclear Power Plants 30MW(e) and over, December 1983

Country	Op'g[a]	Under Construction[b]	Ordered[c]	Total
Argentina	3	1	0	3
Austria	0	1[d]	0	1
Belgium	5	2	0	7
Brazil	0	3	0	3
Bulgaria	4	0	0	4
Canada	13	8	3	24
China	0	0	1	1
Czechoslovakia	3	7	0	10
Egypt	0	2	0	2
Finland	4	0	0	4
France	36	73	2	61
German Democratic Rep.	5	2	0	7
German Federal Rep.	12	10	7	29
Hungary	1	3	0	4
India	4	6	0	10
Iran	0	2	0	2
Iraq	0	0	1	1
Italy	3	6	0	6
Japan	25	11	4	40
Libya	0	0	1	1
Luxembourg	0	0	1	1
Mexico	0	2	0	2
Netherlands	2	0	0	2
Pakistan	1	0	0	1
Philippines	0	1	0	1
Poland	0	0	2	2
Romania	0	3	3	6
South Africa	0	2	0	2
South Korea	3	6	0	9
Spain	5	9	4	17
Sweden	10	2	0	12
Switzerland	4	1	2	7
Taiwan	4	2	0	6
Turkey	0	0	1	1
United Kingdom	33	9	0	42
United States	29	59[e]	2	135
USSR	34	22	6[f]	62
Yugoslavia	1	0	0	1
Total	294	210	34	529

Source: "World List of Nuclear Power Plants," Nuclear News 26 (February 1983): 71-90; and "World List of Nuclear Power Plants," Nuclear News 27 (February 1984): 71-90.

[a] Units in commercial operation.

[b] Includes plants that may be constructed but are not yet in operation; Nuclear News 27 (February 1984): 71-90.

[c] The criterion for listing a unit is either an order or letter of intent signed for the reactor. In cases where the definition of "letter of intent" is ambiguous or where a special situation exists, inclusion depends on judgment of the utility.

[d] A plebisicite has deferred Austria's nuclear energy program indefinitely.

[e] Includes the damaged Three Mile Island reactor.

[f] Insufficient information.

Table 1.2

NUCLEAR GENERATING CAPACITY OUTSIDE THE UNITED STATES

	1981			1982		1985		1990		1995		2000	
	Net MWe Installed	% of Capacity	% of Generation	Net MWe Installed	% of Capacity	Net MWe Installed	% of Capacity	Net MWe Installed	% of Capacity	Net MWe Installed	% of Capacity	Net MWe Installed	% of Capacity
Argentina	344	na	na	344	na	944	8.5	1,642	12.0	2,842	na	3,442	23.0
Austria	0	0	0	0	0	na	na	na	na	na	na	na	na
Belgium	1,666	15.0	25.4	2,566	na	5,427	38.0	na	na	na	na	na	na
Brazil	0	0	0	626	1.5	626	1.2	3,116	4.1	6,851	6.9	10,586	11.0
Bulgaria	1,320	na	na	1,760	na	2,760	na	4,760	35.0	na	na	na	na
Canada	5,498	6.7	10.0	6,131	7.1	10,347	10.5	14,502	13.0	na	na	na	na
China, People's Republic of	0	0	0	0	0	0	0	600	na	3,000	na	16,000	na
Cuba	0	0	0	0	0	0	0	1,320	na	na	na	na	na
Czechoslovakia	880	na	na	880	na	3,080	na	6,280	na	na	na	na	na
Denmark	0	0	0	0	0	0	0	0	0	na	na	na	na
Egypt, Arab Republic of	0	0	0	0	0	0	0	900	6.7	3,600	na	8,400	28.6
Finland	2,160	21.4	35.8	2,160	21.4	2,160	20.0	2,160	19.0	3,160	25.0	na	na
France	21,930	31.0	38.0	23,710	33.0	38,200	43.0	58,000	54.0	na	na	na	85.0
Germany, Democratic Republic of (East)	1,400	na	na	1,400	na	5,360	na	9,000	na	9,000	na	na	50.0
Germany, Federal Republic of (West)	8,856	10.0	14.5	10,081	na	17,700	na	25,000	na	na	na	37,000	50.0
Greece	0	0	0	0	0	0	0	600-900	5.0	na	na	na	na
Hungary	0	0	0	0	0	1,760	na	4,760	10.0	na	na	11,000	48.0
India*	860	2.8	na	860	2.8	1,330	2.8	1,800	3.8	4,415	6.4	10,000	9.3

Table 1.2 (continued)

Country													
Israel	0	0	0	0	0	0	0	0	0	1,900	26.0	4,750	50.0
Italy**	1,424	3.0	1.5	1,273	2.5	1,711	3.6	4,711	6.4	13,711	na	na	na
Japan***	16,077	11.9	16.7	17,177	12.5	25,621	na	46,000	22.0	na	na	90,000	30.0
Korea, Republic of (South)	587	6.0	na	587	6.0	3,815	na	11,215	na	na	na	na	na
Libya	0	0	0	0	0	0	0	na	na	na	na	na	na
Mexico	0	0	0	0	0	654	2.8	1,308	4.0	450	na	na	na
Netherlands, The	505	3.2	7.5	505	3.1	505	3.0	505	na	450	na	450	na
Pakistan	125	na	7.1	125	na	725	na	na	na	na	na	na	na
Philippines, Republic of the	0	0	0	0	0	620	9.5	620	7.9	620	na	620	na
Poland	0	0	0	0	0	0	0	930	na	3,860	na	na	na
Portugal	0	0	0	0	0	0	0	0	0	na	na	2,700	18.0
Romania	0	0	0	0	0	0	0	3,960	20.0	na	na	na	na
South Africa, Republic of	0	0	0	0	na	1,844	7.0	na	na	na	na	na	na
Spain	2,030	6.2	8.6	2,030	na	7,655	20.3	12,555	26.1	18,000	32.1	27,000	40.0
Sweden	4,600	16.8	36.0	6,415	21.0	9,450	30.0	9,450	28.0	na	na	na	na
Switzerland	1,940	13.8	28.1	1,940	13.8	2,882	19.1	na	na	11,578	na	na	na
Taiwan (Republic of China)	2,163	22.4	25.3	3,114	27.3	4,928	31.0	8,728	na	na	na	na	na
Thailand	0	0	0	0	0	0	0	0	0	900	10.1	na	na
Turkey	0	0	0	0	0	0	0	0	0	1,000	na	na	na
Union of Soviet Socialist Republics	15,790	na	na	na	na	na	na	na	na	na	na	na	na
United Kingdom	6,567	9.6	13.4	6,567	9.6	10,267	na	na	na	na	na	na	na
Yugoslavia	632	na	na	632	na	632	na	na	na	na	na	na	na

*Gross MWe.
**Capacity for 1985, 1990 and 1995 includes share of Super Phenix.
***Gross MWe used; 1981 figures, April 1, 1981-March 31, 1982.

Source: Atomic Industrial Forum, INFO News Release (Bethesda, MD: Atomic Industrial Forum, March 1983).

Table 1.3

Forecasts of Installed Nuclear Capacity in OECD Countries (GW)

Regions and Countries	Forecasts for the Year 2000		
	OECD, 1975	INFCE,[a] 1980[b]	OECD, 1982
Western Europe	798	341	214
France	170	96	86
West Germany	134	63	34
United Kingdom	115	33	31
North America	1,115	384	173
Canada	115	59	22
United States	1,000	325	151
Western Pacific	166	130	68
Japan	157	130	68
Australia/New Zealand	--	--	--
Total	2,079	855	455

Source: William Walker and Mans Lönnroth, <u>Nuclear Power Struggles: Industrial Competition and Proliferation Control</u> (London: Allen & Unwin, 1983), p. 48.

[a]INFCE stands for International Fuel Cycle Evaluation.

[b]Figures are averages of high and low estimates.

at the same rate it had in the past. However, worldwide recession in the 1970s, compounded by high interest rates, added to the woes of the nuclear industry. The costs of increasingly lengthy regulatory reviews and extensive safety requirements have placed the nuclear industry in most nations in a serious recession.

However, even assuming present pessimistic growth projections, the capacity of those facilities already installed may increase severalfold by the year 2000. And, although forecasters may have been unduly optimistic in the past, current pessimism about atomic energy's future may be too harsh. As one editorialist recently wrote, "Given the industry's topsy-turvy history, the nuclear future defies prophecy. No one should register surprise if the industry survives a long stay in what looks like its deathbed—and eventually achieves a fairly robust condition."[3]

There are a number of compelling reasons for long-term nuclear power expansion. Clearly fossil fuels are finite and, as in the case of coal, using them raises serious environmental problems. Reliance on oil is doubly uncertain since concentrations of the fuel are located within the domains of unreliable Middle East suppliers. And although electrical demand has slackened, it is certainly not stagnant. Older fossil-fuel plants are nearing retirement and replacement plants must be constructed.

Nuclear power provides convenient answers to the questions raised by such considerations. It diversifies energy resources and it makes the user less vulnerable to external influences. In developing nations, nuclear power is often associated with modernity and is therefore the fuel of choice for new plant construction. And finally, some nations may perceive the peaceful atom as the least obtrusive means of gaining access to weapons-grade material.

There are twenty government-owned and private companies in ten countries—Belgium, Canada, France, West Germany, Italy, Japan, Sweden, the Soviet Union, the United Kingdom, and the United States—serving the nuclear market by manufacturing reactors. Several hundred companies in these and other industrial countries produce reactor-system specialty products such as turbine generators, coolant circulating pumps, containment vessels, valves, pipes, stainless steel castings, and heavy steel plates.[4] Fuel for nuclear plants is processed in large nuclear enrichment complexes in the United States, the Soviet Union, and Europe. Japan and South Africa are also planning commercial-scale facilities. In the European case joint ventures are involved. EURODIF, the European uranium enrichment consortia, includes France, Italy, Spain, and Belgium; URENCO includes West Germany, England, and Holland. Reprocessing plants operate in Belgium, France, India, Italy, Japan, West Germany, the Soviet Union, and the United States. However, most of these reprocessing plants are small and do not contribute significantly to nuclear fuel production.[5]

In the past, nuclear manufacturers have concentrated on domestic markets, but in recent years the market so declined that in the late 1970s a world industry with a capacity to produce 50 to 60 gwe per annum faced a market of only 12 gwe per year.[6] Consequently, manufacturers are now seeking foreign outlets. At the time of this writing five nations export, and provide the training to use, reactors: Canada, France, West Germany, the Soviet Union, and the United States. Japan, with the hope of selling to China, may join this group in the not too distant future. In the longer term developing nations such as India, Argentina, and Brazil may do likewise,[7] entering an increasingly competitive market in which from five to thirty-two export orders are possible by the end of the 1980s.[8] The availability of reactor components from third tier countries such as China, Israel, Romania, South Africa, South Korea, and Spain may make the market even more competitive in the decade to come. Billions of dollars in orders and tens of thousands of jobs will be at stake. Furthermore, the orders may lay the foundation for exports that the industry anticipates for the 1990s as a result of growing energy needs and the replacement market.[9]

Given the economic stakes, exporters are in keen competition, willing to use financing to attract customers. In recent years, France has been the lowest bidder; other exporters have been willing to accept financial losses just to gain a foothold in the market. For example, Germany provided Argentina with a five-year, no-interest loan for its first commercial reactor, plus a subsequent low-interest loan and balance-of-payments considerations. In a sale to Spain, France agreed to cover 90 percent of the financing and to represent Spanish interests in the Common Market. To reduce pressures in importers' foreign exchange and to obtain advantageous trade terms, some exporters have offered barter. France proposed exchanging reactors for Iranian oil and Canada was willing to accept textiles in order to enter the Korean market. West Germany bartered reactors for a discount on Romanian goods. Exporters have used credit with extended and various aid- and export-credit formulas to attract customers.[10] The United States threatened to cut off credit to induce South Korea to import an American reactor.[11]

Since most importers do not produce their own fuel, fuel supplies have been used as a second major buying inducement. American companies told Spain and Yugoslavia that they could not expect U.S. fuel unless they purchased reactors from the United States.[12] (Given U.S. domination of enriched uranium production at the time, the threat was serious.) In one effort to circumvent the American advantage, West Germany included an entire fuel cycle, complete with enrichment and reprocessing facilities, as part of a sale of reactors to Brazil.[13] France sold Pakistan a reprocessing plant (though it later canceled the agreement) and offered another to Korea. Canada competed by offering a reactor that uses natural uranium.

In addition to financing and fuels, exporters use capital costs and design features as sales tools. For example, the natural uranium reactor sold by Canada (the Candu) is 20–30 percent more expensive than the enriched uranium light water reactors sold by other countries and needs scarce and costly heavy water. However, Candu has proven more reliable and runs on cheaper, more readily available natural uranium. The size of reactors is also important. The electrical grids of many developing countries cannot handle the generating capacity of large reactors produced for industrial nations. Complexity of operation is another crucial point for states with limited technical personnel. Safety features, construction time, the availability of parts, and technical advice are additional considerations. For some countries, the reactors' ability to maximize plutonium production (as in the case of Canada's Candu) for fuel or even for weapons purposes may be a major attraction.[14]

The effectiveness of the various inducements is unclear based on the public record, but it is clear that large stakes are involved in the world nuclear market. Even with the decline in growth of electricity consumption, for many nations atomic power is likely to remain an increasingly important resource as their economies grow. The market they will create has important economic implications for exporters in terms of trade balances and healthy domestic nuclear industries.

The Risks

National Diversion

The tie between generation of nuclear energy and manufacture of nuclear weapons by individual states stems from the material that civil nuclear projects produce under the guise of legitimate activities. Plutonium 239 (Pu 239) can be separated from spent reactor fuel.[15] Building a small chemical separation plant for this purpose is not expensive as a national project; estimates range from $18 to $120 million (in 1979 U.S. dollars).[16] Table 1.4 shows that the production of nuclear energy promises large amounts of potential weapons material. The development of fast breeder and high temperature, gas-cooled reactors fueled by Pu 239 and uranium 235 (U 235) will provide additional sources of material, as will reactors using thorium, which breeds fissile uranium 233 (U 233).

An atomic bomb the size of those dropped on Japan requires 5 kilograms of pure plutonium or 15 kilograms of highly enriched uranium.[17] Fabrication should not prove insuperable once weapons material is in hand. Sufficient information is available in open literature, and there are a number of physicists and engineers from many nations who can extrapolate weapons design and methods of fabrication.[18] Still, Pakistan's experience suggests there are substantial technical barriers to overcome that will slow a nation dedicated to producing a weapon.

Fissile material and technical expertise are necessary components to develop nuclear weapons, but motivation is also important.[19] To date nations have shown remarkably great restraint. In the future non-nuclear-armed states may find atom bombs attractive for the same reasons that the United States, Britain, France, China, and the Soviet Union have—namely, strategy, influence, prestige, and bureaucratic reasons. Additional underlying considerations are domestic morale and even economics: As the cost of conventional forces escalates, nuclear weapons may become alternatives. Crises, acquisition of nuclear weapons by rivals, increased availability of fissile material, or successful nuclear demonstrations may become the final precipitant to nuclear power acquisition.[20]

Whether the spread of nuclear weapons undermines or stabilizes international politics has been a matter of debate in scholarly literature. Applying the Soviet-U.S. illustration to other cases, notably that of the Middle East, some scholars have argued that proliferation would result in stabilization.[21] However, most analysts take the contrary view. They contend that we should not be overly sanguine about the Soviet-U.S. relationship proving the case for stability. The superpower relationship is based on

Table 1.4

Estimated Fissile Plutonium Content
of Cumulative Spent Fuel Arisings
(tonnes from January 1978)[1]

Country	1985	1990	2000
EUROPE (EEC)			
Belgium	(4.96)	(10.40)	(27.30)
Denmark	--	--	2.80
France	20.00	52.00	135.00
Germany (Fed. Rep.)	(17.16)	(39.71)	(107.45)
Ireland	--	--	--
Italy	2.06	15.00	*
Luxembourg	--	--	--
Netherlands	(0.77)	(2.45)	(9.82)
United Kingdom	2.50	6.00	29.00
Total	47.00	125.60	311.40
EUROPE (other)			
Austria	(0.55)	(1.10)	(2.20)
Finland	(2.33)	(4.58)	(12.08)
Greece	--	--	--
Iceland	--	--	--
Norway	--	--	--
Portugal	--	(0.42)	(6.01)
Spain	(6.99)	(17.55)	*
Sweden	(7.84)	(15.39)	(28.00)
Switzerland	4.20	8.30	18.80
Turkey	--	--	--
Total	21.90	47.50	69.40
EUROPE Total	69.40	173.10	380.80
NORTH AMERICA			
Canada	(22.35)	(48.79)	(175.65)
United States	(94.00)	(191.50)	(507.00)
Total	164.40	240.30	682.70
PACIFIC AREA			
Australia	--	--	--
Japan	23.00	50.00	200.00
New Zealand	--	--	--
Total	23.00	50.00	200.00
TOTAL OECD	208.70	463.40	1,263.50

Table 1.4 (continued)

Country	1985	1990	2000
NON-OECD			
Argentina	(9.45)	(21.78)	(95.56)
Bangladesh	--	--	(0.02)
Brazil	(0.46)	(4.05)	(38.00)
Egypt	(0.46)	(0.52)	(1.86)
India	(3.45)	(7.52)	(36.49)
Iran	(1.80)	(7.76)	(33.48)
Rep. of Korea	(1.73)	(7.24)	(38.31)
Mexico	(0.45)	(1.51)	(15.34)
Morocco	--	--	(1.10)
Philippines	(0.16)	(0.66)	(2.31)
South Africa	(0.56)	(3.22)	(13.69)
Total	18.50	54.00	276.20
TOTAL	227.20	517.40	1,539.70

Source: International Fuel Cycle Evaluation, Reprocessing, Plutonium Handling Cycle, Report of INFCE Working Group 4 (Vienna, Austria: International Atomic Energy Agency, 1980), pp. 267-268.

1. Parenthetical data estimated from other quantities given (usually by interpolation, e.g., between high and low programs).

*Running stocks for reprocessing plants are not included.

an elaborate, largely unwritten code of conduct that evolved by mutual tacit consent over the last three decades. This code has been reinforced by lengthy consultations and by symmetries in military development. Even with this code, the world was brought to the brink of nuclear war during the 1962 Cuban missile crisis. Although it may be presumptuous to believe that other antagonists could not act with the restraint the Soviets and the United States have generally shown, neither should it be assumed that they will.[22]

In a Hudson Institute report, Lewis Dunn and Herman Kahn suggest that unintended or inadvertent nuclear war could result from a low-level conflict escalating under preemptive pressures, or accidental or unauthorized nuclear attacks. Catalytic war might result from one country attempting to provoke an exchange between two others. Even anonymous nuclear attack is conceivable. History provides numerous examples of first strikes or preventive wars. Finally, the taboo surrounding nuclear weapons may erode and the weapons may be viewed as conventional alternatives.

Dunn and Kahn speculate that along with the increased risk of nuclear war, weapons proliferation is likely to increase global competitiveness and nastiness. The possibility of nuclear black-mail and coercion would increase. Threats to go nuclear may be used for manipulation purposes. Old disputes may be exacerbated. Arms races may result. Confronted by new threats, the superpowers may accelerate their own nuclear programs; they may become increasingly involved in Nth country disputes. Finally, proliferation could result in the undisciplined dissemination of nuclear weapons through sales, gifts, or thefts.[23] Table 1.5 elaborates on these conclusions with examples.

Subnational Diversion and Sabotage

In recent years there has been increasing speculation that subnational groups might find nuclear weapons or nuclear facility sabotage attractive. According to Brian Jenkins, a Rand analyst of international terrorism,

> The rapid growth of a civilian nuclear industry, increasing traffic in plutonium, enriched uranium, and radioactive waste material, the spread of nuclear technology in the United States and abroad—all increase the opportunities for terrorists to engage in some type of "nuclear action." Growing public concern with the potential terrorist threat to nuclear programs and the virtual guarantee of widespread publicity may increase the possibilities that terrorists will attempt such actions.[24]

During the last several years, acts of terrorism, some sponsored by nations rather than by individuals or groups, have increased. Although no terrorist group has demonstrated a nuclear weapons capability, students at Massachusetts Institute of Technology and Princeton University have demonstrated the ability of individuals outside of the government to design on paper what may be credible atom bombs.[25] Threats and acts against nuclear facilities have already taken place. Between 1966 and 1982, 115 threats or incidents of violence occurred against nuclear facilities or offices related in some way to nuclear activities outside the

Table 1.5

Projection of the Problems and Risks of Future Proliferation

Problems or Risks	Some Possible Situations or Cases
A. Risk of Use of Nuclear Weapons	
Inadvertent or unintended nuclear war	Argentina-Brazil Pakistan-India Israel-Arab states Argentina-England
Catalytic nuclear war	PLO-triggered Arab-Israeli war Libya-triggered Syria-Israel war
Anonymous nuclear attack	By Libya, Iraq, Syria, or Iran against Israel By Libya or Iran against U.S. By Soviet Union against U.S.
Terrorist use	Against Israel by PLO fringe Against Western democracies by "Bader-Meinhof" types
Nuclear blitzkriegs or defense against invasion	India-Pakistan South Korea-North Korea Iran-Soviet Union Taiwan-CPR Iraq-Iran
Calculated nuclear first-strike	Israel against Syria India against Pakistan Soviet Union Against Iran Iraq against Iran Iran against Iraq Soviet Union against China
Preventive nuclear war	CPR against Japan Iran against Iraq Iraq against Iran Soviet Union against West Germany South Africa against neighboring states Soviet Union against Yugoslavia
Conventionalization of nuclear weapons	Beginning with preceding small-country nuclear wars and with shifts of Nth country doctrines

Table 1.5 (continued)

Problems or Risks	Some Possible Situations or Cases
B. Increased Global Competitiveness and Nastiness	
Nuclear blackmail and "local Munichs"	Iran against Gulf countries Iraq, Iran, Libya against Israel Israel against Arab state India against Pakistan CPR against Taiwan
Threats to "go" nuclear	Already made by Pakistan, South Korea, and Israel
Exacerbation or rein- vigoration of old disputes	Argentina-Brazil Arab-Israeli dispute Libya-Egypt Iraq-Iran Iran-Saudi Arabia India-Pakistan Japan-CPR Japan-Philippines Indonesia-Philippines England-Argentina
Increased regional arms build-ups	Argentina-Brazil India-Pakistan Israel-Arab states Japan-CPR Japan-Soviet Union Turkey-Greece Iran-Iraq Iran-Saudi Arabia
Superpower confrontations in Nth country disputes	Middle East South Asia Gulf states
Undisciplined dissemination of nuclear weapons	Possible sources: India, Libya, Iran, Iraq, romantic LDC leader brought into control of nuclear weapons by coup d'état

Source: This is my reinterpretation of work by Lewis A. Dunn and Herman Kahn, Trends in Nuclear Proliferation, 1975-1995, HI-2336-RR/3 (Croton-on-Hudson, NY: Hudson Institute, 1976), pp. xxv-xxvi.

United States.[26] Many were not significant, but there were bombings, attempts to breach security, and diversions of nuclear material. Table 1.6 elaborates upon these numbers. Note that perpetrators included the mentally deranged, political terrorists, nuclear power foes, and national separatists. Given the increasing regularity of such events over the years, it is reasonable to conclude that they will continue, possibly with more malevolence.

Thus far no terrorist act has resulted in damage to public health. This fact reflects the difficulty and perhaps the dubious attractiveness of nuclear terrorism. Certainly, a major barrier to subnational nuclear weapons is the inaccessibility of fissile material. It is beyond the means of subnational groups to build isotopic separation facilities; it is barely credible that they could chemically separate Pu 239 from spent fuel. (Spent fuel is highly radioactive and difficult to manipulate under the best of conditions, and it is not easily transportable.)[27] However, should reactors in the future use fuels containing high concentrations of Pu 239 or U 235, subnational groups may find manipulation easier. Unless these materials are heavily guarded or made inaccessible by spiking them with more radioactive products, they could be diverted and fabricated into a crude atom bomb or a radiological weapon that could use aerosol generators or chemical explosives to release materials.

According to the Ford-Mitre study of atomic energy, sabotage of a nuclear power plant would be easier than atom bomb construction. Should saboteurs gain entrance they could use shaped charges to severely damage cooling water conduits, automatic control and safety equipment, and even the primary containment vessel. The resulting possible meltdown might release a substantial fraction of the reactor's contents. The success of sabotage would depend on the saboteurs' familiarity with nuclear plants generally and the target facility specifically, their knowledge of explosives, and most importantly, their ability to breach the facility's defenses.[28]

Even if subnational groups could sabotage atomic plants or fabricate nuclear weapons, there is some question as to whether they would. History suggests that those having the greatest capability are the least likely to use the nuclear option, whereas the "mad bombers" are the least capable yet most likely to do

Table 1.6

Nuclear Activity Outside the U.S.: 1966-1982

Tactic	1966	1968	1973	1974	1975	1976	1977	1978	1979	1980	1981	1982	Total
Bombings	—	—	—	—	5	2	4	5	10	13	15	—	54
Diversion, unauthorized use[a]	—	1	—	—	1	—	—	—	1	1	—	—	4
Theft	1	—	—	1	—	—	—	—	1	1	—	—	4
Sabotage, arson	—	—	—	—	—	—	2	3	4	2	—	—	11
Extortion, threats	—	—	—	—	—	—	—	—	1	—	—	—	1
Insiders	—	—	—	—	—	—	—	—	—	—	—	—	0
Assaults	—	—	1	—	—	—	2	2	2	1	5	1	14
Intrusion, trespass	—	—	—	—	—	—	—	1	2	—	—	—	3
Illegal trade	—	—	—	—	1	—	—	—	—	—	—	—	1
Miscellaneous thefts	—	—	—	3	—	—	—	—	1	1	—	—	5
Malevolent use	—	—	—	—	—	—	3	—	2	1	—	—	6
Unauthorized disclosure	—	—	—	—	—	—	—	—	2	1	—	—	3
Disruption of transport	—	—	—	—	—	—	—	—	1	3	1	—	5
Occupation of facilities	—	—	—	—	—	—	—	—	—	—	—	—	0
Standoff attacks	—	—	—	—	—	—	—	—	—	—	—	1	1
Other	—	—	—	—	—	—	1	—	—	2	—	—	3
Total	1	1	1	4	7	2	12	11	27	26	21	2	115
Number of fatalities	0	0	0	0	0	0	2	2	1	2	2	1	10

Source: Gail Bass and Brian Jenkins, "A Review of Recent Trends in International Terrorism and Nuclear Incidents Abroad," N-1974-SL (Santa Monica, CA: Rand Corporation, 1983), p. 26.

[a]Of nuclear materials.

so. After all, some groups have enough technical knowledge to kill large numbers of people by poisoning water supplies, sabotaging aircraft, or releasing gas, yet they do not. Their reluctance may lie in their assessment that such measures would be counter-productive, causing those they wish to influence to distrust them.[29] However, individuals have engaged in acts of violence that most people would consider irrational. There is some evidence to suggest that even "rational" terrorists are becoming bolder. The apparent sabotage of airliners in the mid-1970s by anti-Castro emigrés and Palestinians, resulting in the deaths of 73 and 88 persons respectively; the deaths of 400 Moslem fanatics in a deliberately set fire in Iran in 1978; and the hundreds of casualties in the bombings of the U.S. Embassy and Marine compound in Beirut in 1983 point in this direction. Yet such incidents tend to represent a tiny fraction of all terrorist actions, and it may be inappropriate to assume that they represent a trend or that they point to the likelihood of nuclear terrorism. Still, given the uncertainties of human behavior, nuclear terrorism cannot be ruled out entirely.[30]

Wartime Destruction

In 1981, Israel destroyed an Iraqi nuclear research reactor because Israeli officials feared that the reactor was a guise for a nuclear weapons program. Policymakers and analysts have paid relatively little attention to the radiological portent of the attack.[31] No radioactive material was released in the raid (nor in an earlier Iranian strike that damaged buildings adjacent to the reactor at the outset of the war with Iraq nor in attacks by Iraq on Iran's nuclear plants in 1984 and 1985) because the reactor was not yet in operation. Even if the reactor had been "hot," it is questionable that the contamination would have been significant given its small size.[32] However, had the installation been a nuclear power plant, which customarily generates sixty times the energy of Baghdad's plant, contamination would have been significant had a substantial fraction of the radioactive core been released.[33] Column B in Table 1.7 shows land contamination resulting from a conventional weapons-attack-induced meltdown of a large power reactor analogous to

Table 1.7

Area in Square Miles Affected by Nuclear Energy Facilities Release Scenarios[a]

Time Unhabitable	A 1 Megaton Weapon	B Reactor (1000 Mwe) Meltdown[b]	C Weapon on Reactor	D Weapon on Waste Stor. Facility
1 week	31,000	2,200 (5,300)[c]	79,000	113,000
2 weeks	26,000	2,000	72,000	110,000
1 month	21,000	1,800	64,000	103,000
2 months	17,000	1,600	54,000	100,000
6 months	5,000	1,200	33,000	83,000
1 year	1,200	900	25,000	67,000
2 years	150	680	17,000	49,000
5 years	11	320	10,000	35,000
10 years	2	140 (550-4,300)	6,000	30,000
20 years	1	68	3,200	25,000
50 years		50 (240-3,300)	1,200	14,000
100 years		20	180	2,400

Sources: Steve Fetter and Kosta Tsipis, "Catastrophic Nuclear Radiation Releases" (Cambridge, MA, Program in Science and Technology for International Security, Department of Physics, Report No. 5, September 1980), Tables 2, 3, 6, 8. Figures in parentheses are from Jan Beyea, "Some Long-Term Consequences of Hypothetical Major Releases of Radioactivity to the Atmosphere from Three Mile Island" (Princeton, NJ, Princeton University Center for Energy and Environmental Studies, PU/CEES No. 109), p. B-13.

[a]Fetter and Tsipis assume that an area becomes uninhabitable for a given time assuming the maximum allowable dose is 2 REM per year.

[b]For elaboration see Bennett Ramberg, Destruction of Nuclear Energy Facilities in War: The Problem and the Implications (Lexington, MA: Lexington Books, 1980), pp. 13-70; and U.S. Nuclear Regulatory Commission, Reactor Safety Study, WASH 1400 (Springfield, VA: National Technical Information Service, 1975), appendix VI. Note these calculations assume major release of radiation akin to a PWR 2 defined in the Reactor Safety Study. Releases of lesser magnitudes are possible. The extensiveness of a conventional weapons-induced release is a product of numerous variables including the effectiveness of the bombardment to disrupt reactor systems designed to contain releases, the quantity and quality of material entering the atmosphere, weather, topography, and rate of deposition. For the implications of late containment failure in reducing releases see American Physical Society,"Report to the American Physical Society Study Group on Radionuclide Release from Severe Accidents at Nuclear Power Plants," draft, February 1985. In military bombardment early containment failure resulting in large releases is conceivable.

[c]The figures in parentheses are drawn from Beyea, cited in source note. They "assume that occupation would be restricted if the resident population would otherwise receive more than a 10 REM whole body radiation dose over 30 years. This corresponds to about a three-fold increase over the natural background dose in the same period. A ten REM whole body dose has associated with it a risk of a .05 to .5 percent chance of cancer death."

a major accident. Note that one week after the release 2,200 square miles could be contaminated. (A more conservative calculation of health risks to exposures of 10 rem over a thirty-year period extends the zone of concern to 5,300 square miles.) Two years after the meltdown the radioactive debris of a power reactor can contaminate more land than that of a one-megaton nuclear weapon (680 square miles versus 150 square miles). The problem is compounded when the contents of several reactors on one site are released as a result of attack, which is conceivable in wartime scenarios. Column C defines contamination caused by detonation of a one-megaton nuclear weapon on a large power reactor. Reflecting the longer-lived radiation contained in the reactor, the addition of the radioactivity of the reactor's core to that of the weapon could threaten 79,000 square miles versus 31,000 square miles by the weapon alone one week after the attack. After one year, twenty-five times more land would remain contaminated by a weapon and reactor in combination than by a weapon alone. Column D illustrates that the problem is significantly worse when a nuclear weapon destroys a large waste storage facility.

Some of the implications of the military destruction of an atomic plant were laid out by Britain's Royal Commission on Environmental Pollution:

> We have given some thought to the possible effects of war so far as nuclear installations are concerned; these installations, providing vital energy supplies, would be prime targets. In a nuclear war the effects of attack on nuclear installations would be one part of the general catastrophe, but an attack with conventional weapons leading to the release of radioactivity would produce some of the effects of nuclear weapons. Quantities of fission products could be released and they would not be carried into the stratosphere.
>
> The effects of war, even of "conventional" war, are inevitably horrifying, but if these effects could be magnified by attacks on nuclear installations, then this is a major factor to consider whether, or to what extent, to use nuclear power. This threat also exists, and should likewise be weighed, in the non-nuclear field. The vast increase in the chemical process industry over the last few decades has created many industrial plants where

dangerous substances are used or stored and where the consequences of damage from armed attack could be extremely serious. The unique aspect of nuclear installations is that the effects of the radioactive contamination that could be caused are so long-lasting. If nuclear power could have been developed earlier, and had it been in widespread use at the time of the last war, it is likely that some areas of central Europe would still be uninhabitable because of ground contamination by caesium.[34]

Given these consequences why would any nation destroy a nuclear plant? Beyond the Israeli rationale—namely, to prevent an adversary's acquisition of atomic weapons, an alternative contemplated by the Russians in the 1960s as they pondered China's nuclear arsenal and by the United States in the 1950s as it looked upon the growing Soviet nuclear arsenal with concern—there are a number of reasons. In recent conflicts including World War II, Korea, Vietnam, and the Middle East wars, combatants have targeted enemy energy sources in order to cripple the opponent's industrial capabilities to wage war. Destruction of the environment for military purposes also has precedents. The Dutch destroyed their dikes during World War II in order to hamper the Germans. The Soviet Union followed a scorched-earth policy for the same reason. During the Vietnam War, the United States employed herbicides to destroy enemy defensive cover and to improve target identification.

Furthermore, nuclear plants may be threatened or destroyed because they represent one of the greatest concentrations of capital investment a country is likely to possess. A party with a stake in an ongoing conflict between two countries may consider sabotaging a facility to escalate the conflict. Since many people in many countries are now acutely concerned about the possible release of radionuclides from power plants, a belligerent antagonist could threaten radioactive contamination as a means of coercion.[35]

Accidents

Of the five nuclear risks, an accident at a power plant has been the most extensively debated. Unless the heat generated by the reactor is removed, the reactor core melts, breaching its containment shell and releasing radioactive material into the environment. Meltdowns can be caused by coolant-pipe breaks, vessel ruptures, and uncontrolled fission, resulting in an over-heated core. The probability of a major reactor accident has been variously estimated at one in 10,000 per reactor year to as low as one in 200,000.[36] Accidents can also release materials from spent fuel storage areas, reprocessing plants, waste depositories, and fuel fabrication facilities, although mathematical probabilities in these areas remain undefined.

Damage to the environment from any nuclear release depends on the volume of vented material, its composition, rate of deposition, weather conditions, geography, population density, and civil defense. Contamination from major reactor accidents could cover thousands of square miles, as shown in Table 1.7. Some fuel-cycle accidents could be even more damaging. Health consequences depend on the intensity and duration of exposure, the type of organ exposed, and sex and age of the individual, with greater exposure increasing chances of early and late fatalities and genetic effects. Fortunately, to date the world has been spared a major reactor accident, although a nuclear "incident" of unexplained origins occurred in the Ural Mountains in 1957, contaminating hundreds of square miles and leaving much of the region permanently uninhabitable.[37]

Conclusions

The nuclear weapons club has not expanded in recent years, and thus far, the consequences of subnational nuclear terrorism have been benign. No nuclear installation in operation has been threatened or attacked in time of war. And save for the Urals incident, no major accident has significantly contaminated the environment. Still, the risks posed by the presence of nuclear energy persist and expand as facilities and materials multiply around the world.

2
Current Treatment

Four principal international accords currently address nuclear security risks: the Non-Proliferation Treaty, International Atomic Energy Agency (IAEA) safeguards, nuclear suppliers agreements, and the 1977 Protocol Additional to the Geneva Conventions on the law of war. These are supplemented by regional European and Latin American treaties, bilateral safeguards agreements between exporters and importers, and the work of the International Nuclear Fuel Cycle Evaluation (INFCE). Collectively these accords and their associated institutions form an international nuclear energy regime—a set of norms to which most nations adhere. The underlying principle of this regime is that atomic energy makes an important contribution toward meeting the world's needs, but that this contribution should not imperil the world by the risks identified in the previous chapter. Accordingly, the international community has committed itself to insure that plants are operated safely for peaceful purposes. Although each of the institutions listed above contributes toward minimization of nuclear risks, each also manifests significant inadequacies in applying preventive measures.

The Non-Proliferation Treaty

The Non-Proliferation Treaty (NPT) entered into force in 1970 commits non-nuclear-weapons signatories to avoid acquiring, controlling, or manufacturing nuclear weapons or other explosive nuclear devices. To verify compliance the parties agree to negotiate IAEA inspections and other safeguards. The treaty also stipulates that all parties, including nuclear weapons states, agree to exchange equipment, materials, and information on the peaceful utilization of nuclear energy. The treaty allows states to work for arms control or to withdraw under extraordinary circumstances.[1]

The NPT has gained wide acceptance—as Table 2.1 shows, as of October 1983 it had 121 non-nuclear state parties, in addition to 3 nuclear armed nations, the United Kingdom, the United States, and the Soviet Union, but not the 2 remaining official members of the nuclear weapons club, China and France. Of the non-signatories, the nuclear ambitions of 6 nations have been of particular concern to the integrity of the non-proliferation regime: India, which exploded a "peaceful" nuclear device in 1974; Pakistan, which may be endeavoring to match the Indian effort; Israel, which may already have nuclear weapons produced with materials from its Dimona research reactor; South Africa, which has a nuclear energy program including fuel-cycle facilities; and Argentina and Brazil, both of which are developing important nuclear fuel-cycle capabilities.

Although member states are committed not to manufacture nuclear weapons or weapons devices under the NPT, anything short of actual assembly is not forbidden, which many see as a dangerous loophole. Threatening to develop nuclear weapons is not prohibited. The term "nuclear explosive devices" is not defined. Safeguards apply to peaceful nuclear facilities but not to military installations.[2] Finally, the escape clause declares that a signatory need give the United Nations Security Council only three months' notice that withdrawal is necessary because of "extraordinary events" that "have jeopardized the supreme interests" of a country.

International Atomic Energy Agency Safeguards

Agency Efforts to Stem the Spread of Nuclear Weapons

The success of the nuclear regime depends on self-enforcement strengthened by international safeguards. To verify that non-nuclear-weapons states do not divert nuclear material to weapons, the IAEA operates two types of safeguards—one for NPT

Table 2.1

Parties to the Non-Proliferation Treaty[a]

1. Afghanistan[b]	49. Ireland
2. Antigua and Barbuda (1 April 83)	50. Italy
3. Australia	51. Ivory Coast
4. Austria	52. Jamaica
5. Bahamas (10 January 75)	53. Japan
6. Bangladesh	54. Jordan
7. Barbados (21 August 81)	55. Kenya (5 March 72)
8. Belgium	56. Korea, Republic of
9. Benin (30 April 74)	57. Laos People's Democratic
10. Bolivia[c] (5 March 72)	Republic (5 March 72)
11. Botswana (5 March 72)	58. Lebanon
12. Bulgaria	59. Lesotho
13. Burundi (19 September 72)	60. Liberia (5 March 72)
14. Canada	61. Libyan Arab Jamahiriya
15. Cape Verde (24 April 81)	62. Liechtenstein
16. Central African Republic	63. Luxembourg
(25 April 72)	64. Madagascar
17. Chad (10 September 72)	65. Malaysia
18. Congo (23 April 80)	66. Maldives, Republic of
19. Costa Rica	67. Mali (5 March 72)
20. Cyprus	68. Malta (5 March 72)
21. Czechoslovakia	69. Mauritius
22. Democratic Kampuchea	70. Mexico
(2 December 73)	71. Mongolia
23. Democratic Yemen (1 December 80)	72. Morocco
24. Denmark	73. Nauru (7 December 83)
25. Dominican Republic	74. Nepal
26. Ecuador	75. Netherlands
27. Egypt	76. New Zealand
28. El Salvador	77. Nicaragua
29. Ethiopia	78. Nigeria (5 March 82)
30. Fiji	79. Norway
31. Finland	80. Panama (13 July 78)
32. Gabon[c] (7 August 75)	81. Papua New Guinea
33. Gambia	82. Paraguay
34. German Democratic Republic	83. Peru
35. Germany, Federal Republic of	84. Philippines
36. Ghana	85. Poland
37. Greece	86. Portugal
38. Grenada (19 February 76)	87. Romania
39. Guatemala	88. Rwanda (20 November 76)
40. Guinea-Bissau (20 February 76)	89. St. Lucia (29 June 81)
41. Haiti[c] (2 June 72)	90. Samoa
42. Holy See	91. San Marino[c] (5 March 72)
43. Honduras	92. Senegal
44. Hungary	93. Sierra Leone[c] (26 August 76)
45. Iceland	94. Singapore
46. Indonesia	95. Solomon Islands
47. Iran, Islamic Republic of	(17 December 82)
48. Iraq	96. Somalia (5 March 72)

Table 2.1 (continued)

97. Sri Lanka^c (5 September 80)	110. Uganda (20 April 84)
98. Sudan	111. United Kingdom
99. Surinam	112. United States
100. Swaziland	113. United Republic of Cameroon
101. Sweden	(5 March 72)
102. Switzerland	114. Upper Volta (5 March 72)
103. Syrian Arab Republic	115. Uruguay
(5 March 72)	116. USSR
104. Thailand	117. Venezuela
105. Togo (5 March 72)	118. Viet Nam (14 December 83)
106. Tongo^c (7 January 73)	119. Yugoslavia
107. Tunisia (5 March 72)	120. Zaire
108. Turkey	121. Republic of China
109. Tuvalu (19 July 80)	(5 March 72)

Source: International Atomic Energy Agency, International Atomic Energy
Agency Bulletin 25 (December 1983).

^aAs of 13 October 1983, the International Atomic Energy Agency had negotiated
safeguards agreements with 83 non-nuclear-weapon states party to the NPT.
Safeguards agreements were in force with 76 of these states. Safeguards
agreements with 7 more non-nuclear-weapon states that had been approved by
the IAEA Board of Governors were awaiting entry into force. The date in
parentheses after the name of the state indicates the time by which the
NPT safeguards agreement should have entered or should enter into force.

^bUnderscored states have an NPT safeguards agreement in force.

^cSafeguards agreement approved by the IAEA Board of Governors and awaiting
entry into force.

signatories and another for non-signatories. Both apply the
principle that the way to deter diversion is to ensure early
detection. Non-NPT safeguards apply to installations voluntarily
designated by the state to prevent their use "to further any
military purposes," and include accounting for nuclear material,
inspecting sites by IAEA personnel, and equipping installations
with surveillance and containment devices. By contrast, NPT
safeguards apply to *all* nuclear material and facilities located
in a state. Their purpose is to insure that fissionable materials
are "not diverted to nuclear weapons or other nuclear explosive
devices," thus eliminating the ambiguity of the non-NPT codification, which could have been interpreted to allow peaceful
nuclear explosives. As of 1983 safeguard agreements were in
force in seventy-six nations with seven others waiting to be
approved by the IAEA Board of Governors.[3]

On the average inspections take place six times per year and
involve ten to fifteen staff days per annum per reactor. Inspections

include auditing accounting and operating records, verifying fresh fuels prior to loading, and counting fuel assemblies in the core. After the reactor is operating, surveillance equipment monitors installations continually, usually via 8-millimeter movie cameras and video systems operating on a time-lapse basis. Other surveillance devices also monitor materials in transit, including loading and unloading ports and spent fuel storage areas. The agency has had camera-reliability problems, which are being remedied; cameras are now constructed to implode if tampered with. The agency also has developed special door seals to monitor storage areas where sensitive nuclear material is kept. Wire seals are being replaced by more reliable tamper-proof coded fiber-optic devices. In 1980 about 600 seals were issued and 6,000,000 surveillance pictures were taken, with 3,000 returned for verification. Agency inspectors submitted reports on about 500 nuclear plants and about 400,000 data entries were made on agency computers.[4]

How effective are these agency safeguards? The intensity of the debate on this question indicates many perceptions of the inherent deficiencies in the rights of inspectors, in the inspectorate, and in accounting methods. Safeguards are intended to be as non-intrusive as possible—they should not hamper a state's economic and technological development, for if they did, it might provide a rationale for disregarding the safeguards. And therein lies their weakness. Matters are further complicated by inspectors who are academically qualified but largely inexperienced: Many have never worked in nuclear installations and must obtain their experience on the job. Naturally, it takes time before they become fully effective. But the agency has no career system for inspectors. Most inspectors leave within a few years, often due to the stressful nature of the job, so their period of optimal effectiveness is limited. Furthermore, the IAEA has not established performance standards: Some inspectors take an adversary approach, while others are more lenient. There are also the inevitable cases of incompetence.[5]

Accounting problems result from the fact that the measurement can never be 100 percent accurate, although better instrumentation could improve results. During fabrication, nuclear materials undergo chemical conversions and mechanical and heat treatment, all of which contribute to operational losses of 1 percent to 2 percent. This loss often involves dust lodged in ventilation systems and operating equipment and particles washed away by waste processes. A 1 percent material loss is common during shipment, given that the moisture content of substances changes and that small amounts of powder or gas are "gained" or "lost" because of differences in measuring instruments and techniques. The accuracy of estimating the number of U 238 atoms that become Pu 239 varies from one reactor design to another by as much as plus or minus 5 percent. Finally, there is genuine material unaccounted for (MUF). As more nuclear material is processed, the real amounts of losses of all kinds could become substantial.[6]

Does the agency use the tools available to it? How effective are they? In order to protect national proprietary interests, reports by the inspectorate are not published. According to the agency's charter, should violations be uncovered, the director general—the organization's principal administrator—is advised. He, in turn, informs the board of governors, the institution's governing body, which has authority to request remedial action. He must also advise the United Nations Security Council and General Assembly. If compliance is not forthcoming, the board of governors may suspend or curtail IAEA aid and demand return of exported material and equipment supplied by the organization.

In 1975, after reviewing agency methods, the U.S. General Accounting Office concluded that

> The real effectiveness of IAEA safeguards is not known. There is no public evidence to show whether IAEA safeguards have prevented or detected diversion of nuclear materials from intended purposes. The mere fact that the IAEA has never disclosed a diversion is not sufficient assurance to many countries that IAEA safeguards are effective. Effective international safeguards depend in large measure on the intent and cooperation of the country to which they are applied and the adequacy of technological control and implementation. However, technological control in the absence of genuine political commitment is inadequate. IAEA officials have stated that safeguards would never

be completely effective—they could never be fully confident that no material has been diverted. U.S. and IAEA officials generally conceded that a country could circumvent safeguards if it was willing to assume the risk of detection, incur the expense, and take the trouble to do so.[7]

Following publication of the comptroller general's report, the Nuclear Regulatory Commission (NRC), the Department of State, and the Energy Research and Development Administration (ERDA), in separate reports, equated the organization's effectiveness with its theoretical capabilities and declared the agency effective. This conclusion was reinforced by the fact that U.S. personnel were employed by the agency's inspectorate. The agency did publicly acknowledge at least one case of diversion in the 1970s: In 1975 .5 kilogram of enriched uranium was reported missing from an undisclosed facility. And in the last two years the agency announced that it was unable to verify the integrity of the safeguards on heavy water reactors in South Asia. The fact that the agency has never made other announcements, according to the NRC, Department of State, and ERDA, reflects the absence of anything to report.[8]

Each of these U.S. government departments, including the NRC, was disposed, at least prior to the Carter administration, toward promoting nuclear energy. Whether or not this disposition colored their assessment of the IAEA is uncertain. However, there is some support for the comptroller general's pessimism. In October 1977, the IAEA reported on a number of "problem areas" concerning the application of controls. The study found that in 1976 the IAEA was unable to verify adherence to safeguards in ten out of forty-one countries where they were applied. The accounting methods used by several countries produced artificially low estimates of uranium and plutonium lost in processing, making it "difficult or impossible to draw valid conclusions . . . regarding the possibility that a diversion has occurred."[9] There were instances where storage arrangements did not always permit physical access by inspectors. In one case a large inventory of irradiated fuel containing plutonium could not be verified because it was inaccessible in a spent fuel cooling pond. In another, a general lack of data prevented inspectors from determining if diversions of material had taken place.[10]

These problems have continued into the 1980s. At the beginning of this decade, twenty-seven countries submitted the required inventory reports up to two months late. Of greater concern, 12 percent of the nuclear facilities had surveillance-camera failures. In 1982 the agency acknowledged that on the average 200 anomalies, that is, unusual, observable conditions, were found in inspected plants per year. However, most, it said, were readily resolved.[11]

Analysts outside the agency have questioned its effectiveness, but perhaps the greatest indictment of IAEA safeguards came in the congressional testimony of Roger Richter, an IAEA inspector, following Israel's strike against Iraq's nuclear reactor in 1981. Richter described safeguard anomalies generally and specifically with regard to the Osirak reactor. He decried host nations having the right to veto inspectors on the basis of their nationality, the presumption being that investigators from friendly countries are more willing to overlook irregularities. In Richter's words, "As an accepted inspector, you must keep in mind that any adverse conclusions you might reach as a result of your inspections would have to take into account your country's sensitivity to how this information might affect relations. . . ."[12] Thus, in the case of Iraq, only inspectors from the Soviet Union, Hungary, and France were allowed on site. Also, inspections take place only once every four months for an inoperative reactor (more frequently after start up) and require advance notification; the host country can delay further to cover up irregularities.

Richter's greatest complaint focused on the scope of inspection.[13] Only facilities designated by the host nation to contain thorium; natural, enriched, or depleted uranium in metal or oxide form; or plutonium are open to inspection. In the Iraqi case, investigators had to ignore hot cells provided by Italy that could process plutonium, a radiochemistry lab, and 200,000 pounds of uranium acquired from Portugal. Because the Iraqi plant was a research reactor, surveillance cameras were not present to photograph the loading and unloading of nuclear material. Even if the cameras had been in place, their effectiveness would have been diminished because test reactors such as Osirak are subject to frequent experiments in which specimens for radioactive bombardment are inserted in the core and later withdrawn. Such experiments could serve as a guise to irradicate fuel to produce plutonium.

However, the inspector's job is not superfluous. He does check accounting records. Unirradiated fuel is subject to physical inspection to establish that the elements containing enriched uranium fuel—which itself, if highly enriched, can serve as the feedstock for nuclear weapons—are not replaced by dummy elements. Irradiated fuel elements can be visually inspected with the reactor running to confirm that the elements are not dummies. This facet of inspection, according to Richter, is the easiest; "the most difficult part lies ahead."

> You, the inspector, will now return to Vienna and report that your inspection disclosed no discrepancies between the operator's and that of the Agency. You will report that you verified the unirradiated fuel with your stabilized assay meter by virtue of seeing the reactor in operation. The difficult part of the job is that you must prepare yourself mentally to ignore the many signs that may indicate the presence of clandestine activities going on in the facilities adjacent to the reactor, facilities you were not permitted to inspect unless the host country has informed you that fuel elements from the reactor were transferred there. You will now complete a standard report filling in the blanks, you will try to forget that you have just been party to a very misleading process.[14]

His criticisms notwithstanding, Richter does not believe that the IAEA's goals are hopeless. Indeed, he concludes "there is no other viable substitute for the IAEA," but the agency must be allowed greater authority by its members to fulfill its mandate. He counsels each member nation to ask "whether its security and the collective security of the world community will be better served by improving the confidence and respect for the IAEA, or whether unbridled proliferation and short term commercial advantages should take precedence."[15]

The agency's defense of its performance in Baghdad was as adamant as its former employee's criticism. H. Gruemm, deputy director general of safeguards for the IAEA, criticized Richter for making judgments without personal knowledge of the reactor.[16] Richter himself had never made an on-site inspection of the plant. Grumm argued that agency safeguards were adequate to detect either the removal of enriched uranium-bearing fuel elements or the blanketing of the reactor core to produce plutonium. He declared that Richter in his testimony was "careful enough not to mention the necessary, drastic, and easily observable changes of reactor configuration and the strong dependence of plutonium production on supply of fuel by France. He forgot to mention that facilities in Iraq not yet submitted to safeguards would have come under safeguards when they first contained nuclear material. . . ."[17]

Richter's contentions and those of his detractors cannot be resolved here; we simply do not have enough data to date. In Richter's defense, earlier General Accounting Office documentation and other congressional testimony suggest that he is certainly not alone in his skepticism.[18] However, there is also evidence to suggest that the agency will not back away from reporting suspicions about safeguard violations. In late 1981 the IAEA acknowledged that it could no longer determine whether Pakistan was diverting nuclear material for military purposes from the safeguarded Kanupp reactor.[19]

IAEA Efforts to Ensure Nuclear Safety

The IAEA does not limit the application of preventive medicine to non-proliferation safeguards; it also plays a role in facility safety and physical security. But its role is limited to advising only, to preserve individual nation's sovereignty. The agency has promulgated voluntary guidelines for states to employ to prevent theft or sabotage. They include limiting access to authorized personnel; using physical barriers, alarms, guards, and emergency procedures; and protecting nuclear material in transit.[20] These have been recently reinforced by an international convention on the physical protection of nuclear material in transit from country to country.[21] The IAEA also publishes a series of safety guidelines dealing with regulatory responsibilities, nuclear facility siting, design and operation, and quality assurance.[22] Member states of the agency have given it no authority to enforce any of these provisions.

The safety imperative was highlighted by the 1979 Three Mile Island reactor accident. The idea that safety is a matter of international concern rests on the fact that in many regions, nuclear plants are located near national boundaries. One quarter of the plants represented in the Organization for Economic Cooperation and Development (OECD) are within 40 kilometers of a border. Even leaving aside Three Mile Island, the operating competency of the nuclear industry leaves much to be desired. Anomalies in the performance of U.S. reactors are well documented.[23] The problems in the remainder of the world, particularly in developing countries, are less well known, but have been illuminated in congressional testimony.

Regulatory organization in the less developed nations using nuclear power is subminimal; most regulatory agencies are understaffed and often the personnel are inexperienced. A professor of nuclear engineering at the State University of New York described South Korea's regulatory agency staff in the following terms: "They discussed sincerely all the problems, but you could feel the lack of experience. They knew they had to have a concept of quality assurance and safety, but they didn't have the manpower."[24] Similar problems were pointed out in the Philippines and Yugoslavia. Many nations rely on foreign consultants, including IAEA representatives, but often their recommendations are ignored. Though agency inspectors of Mexico's Laguna Verde nuclear plant identified several problems during one inspection, they returned to Mexico to find their remedial recommendations had all been largely neglected.

Another problem in maintaining safety standards is manifest in poorly sited plants. Brazil's Agra facility is situated in an earthquake zone and subject to dangerous tidal action for which design does not compensate. In the Philippines a plant is being constructed near a dormant volcano.[25] Perhaps the clearest example of poor regulation is India's plant, where maintenance personnel are subject to excessive doses of radiation due to the improper construction of the facility. Thus although the IAEA has progressed in developing nuclear safety standards, its most important challenge lies in enforcing these standards—a difficult task, inasmuch as the IAEA has no real power to do so.

The Suppliers Group Guidelines

In 1974 the United States, Canada, France, West Germany, Japan, the United Kingdom, and the Soviet Union met secretly to review what nuclear suppliers could do to ensure the peaceful use of nuclear energy. The suppliers group—later enlarged to include Belgium, Czechoslovakia, East Germany, Italy, the Netherlands, Poland, Sweden, and Switzerland—negotiated in 1976 several voluntary, non-binding agreements establishing guidelines for the sale of nuclear facilities. In so doing it expanded upon a list adopted by the Nuclear Exporters Committee—the Zangger Committee—established in 1970 by a dozen industrialized nations to interpret the NPT safeguards clause. The updated guidelines stipulate that suppliers should sell only nuclear materials and equipment that would trigger application of IAEA safeguards. The criteria also require that recipients agree not to build nuclear explosive devices, and exporters and importers mutually consent upon physical security, which becomes the responsibility of the recipient only. Suppliers agreed to exercise "restraint" in transferring "sensitive facilities, technology, and weapons-usable materials." Importers were encouraged to accept multinational reprocessing and enrichment centers rather than build domestic plants. The agreement also stipulates that transfers should not be made unless the importer agrees that in case of retransfer the recipient would be bound by the assurances the first transferee had assumed and that transactions involving designated sensitive material be approved by the original supplier.[26]

The voluntary supplier guidelines are important because no behavior standards had theretofore existed in nuclear trade. Such standards held hope that suppliers would constrain their use of potentially dangerous inducements to gain orders, but they engendered skepticism as well. The Stockholm International Peace Research Institute (SIPRI) represented the guidelines as "essentially a gentlemen's agreement" rather than a treaty: a document without legal authority.[27] Both hope and skepticism have persisted into the 1980s.

In a large sense the guidelines provided quasi codification for the status quo in relations between exporters. Still, large loopholes allowed the more aggressive exporters to pursue customers with some of the gusto of the past, and some arrangements did tramp upon the spirit, if not the letter, of the guidelines. In 1979 West Germany and Switzerland provided Argentina with a reactor and heavy water, respectively, without requiring Argentina to apply full-scope safeguards. In 1981, France, West Germany, and the United States negotiated with Mexico over the transfer of enrichment technology as a part of a drive to attract major reactor contracts, while Cuba, a non-NPT country, bought a reactor from the Soviet Union without comprehensive safeguards. In 1982 Canada discussed the export of reactors to Kuwait and Saudi Arabia—both non-NPT countries—while France talked to another non-NPT country, Israel, about purchasing a reactor. The United States continued to supply fuel to the Indians until congressional pressure forced the administration to relent, but not before the United States had entered into an agreement by which France would fulfill the obligation.[28] (However, it must be acknowledged, the United States preserved safeguards at Tarapur. Had the United States simply broken its supply agreement, India would have been free of any safeguard obligation.)

Such behavior led William Walker and Mans Lönnroth, authors of probably the best study of the international nuclear market today, to conclude that some loosening of trade standards has occurred, reversing the trend towards a tighter market that characterized the second half of the 1970s.[29] Loosening, however, is not the same as abandoning, and exporters today are more cautious; notably, they no longer use enrichment or reprocessing plants to sweeten a sale. This change seems to reverse a pattern that culminated in West Germany's agreement to provide an entire fuel cycle to Brazil. Even in sales promised to sensitive regions, there is new caution. France, although consenting to rebuild Iraq's research reactor, will no longer permit it to be fueled with highly enriched, weapons-grade uranium.[30]

International Nuclear Fuel Cycle Evaluation

In 1977 the United States initiated the International Nuclear Fuel Cycle Evaluation (INFCE), a study of alternatives to advanced fuel cycles using plutonium and highly enriched uranium. Although a number of countries feared that the United States might use the study as an opportunity to impose its preferences, sixty-six nations and five international organizations participated.[31] Although the conference did not fulfill all of President Carter's hopes, it afforded an opportunity to sensitize nations to the proliferation dangers of certain technologies and to discourage implementation of such technologies. Eight working groups were established to study fuel and heavy water availability, enrichment availability, supply assurances, reprocessed plutonium handling and recycling fast breeders, spent fuel management, waste management and disposal, and advanced fuel cycle and reactor concepts.

The forum did achieve many U.S. objectives, but its optimal hopes were not realized. There was uncertainty regarding availability of uranium stocks and enrichment services, and the desire for greater energy independence appears to have overridden U.S. attempts to preclude commercialization of plutonium-based fuels and the breeder. The conference also failed to find a technical fix to protect plutonium from diversion. Still, some participants agreed that concern over plutonium diversion is legitimate, and states advocating early reprocessing and breeders were on the defensive. Furthermore, there was a consensus that breeders require an economy of scale and thus should be large, limited in number, and closely safeguarded. For most countries reliance on international markets was preferable from both the economic and the security perspective. Finally, participants agreed that plutonium should be controlled by an international regime using more advanced safeguards. One U.S. Department of Energy participant concluded that "it seems likely that INFCE's main accomplishment will have been to better sensitize nations to the broader implications of technological, economic, and political choices in nuclear energy development, and to have set in motion a number of processes of consultation and institution-building that will undoubtedly outlive the study and could have an important role in shaping influence on the future nuclear energy regime."[32]

The Geneva Protocol Additional

One failure of the world's nuclear regime is the unwillingness of nations to forbid attacks on nuclear plants. The 1977 Protocol Additional to the Geneva Conventions of 12 August 1949, relating to the Protection of Victims of International Armed Conflicts (Protocol I, which defines the laws of war), addresses the legitimacy of wartime destruction of nuclear power plants. The document is a mixture of ambiguity and contradiction. It prohibits the destruction of a power plant if it would result in "severe" losses among civilian life, but there is no definition of what constitutes severity. Equally confusing is a stipulation allowing the destruction of nuclear power plants if they provide electric power "in regular, significant, and direct support of military operations," which is in direct conflict with another provision mandating that "care" be taken to protect the environment "against widespread, long-term, and severe damage."[33]

In addition, the codification is restrictively applied. The document neglects large depositories of radionuclides located at reprocessing plants, spent fuel and waste storage facilities, and fuel fabrication installations recycling plutonium or U 233. It fails to address the legitimacy of a belligerent destroying its own facilities, releasing radionuclides in order to make combat more difficult for an adversary. It also overlooks threats to destroy facilities as a legitimate means of coercion. If destruction is prohibited, consistency requires that threats likewise be banned.

The 1981 Israeli strike on Iraq's reactor stimulated the UN-sponsored Committee on Disarmament to take up the matter in the context of radiological weapons, about which it has been negotiating since 1979. Sweden, which first raised the issue even prior to the bombing, declared that the only effective way radiological elements could be introduced into conflict apart from nuclear weapons was through military destruction of atomic plants. All efforts to ban such attacks have foundered on the comprehensiveness of the issue. Some nations argue that a prohibition should include all nuclear installations whether military or civilian, while others would ban attacks on civilian nuclear plants only.[34]

Regional and Bilateral Safeguards

In addition to global efforts to ensure the peaceful utilization of nuclear energy, steps have been taken regionally and bilaterally. The European Atomic Energy Community (EURATOM) has made the most significant regional effort in early detection safeguards. EURATOM was founded in 1957 to promote and integrate Europe's nuclear energy programs. Its original members included Belgium, West Germany, France, Italy, Luxembourg, and the Netherlands. Although the organization never fully attained integration,[35] it did sponsor several cooperative undertakings, including an inspection system to ensure that "ores, source materials, and special fissionable materials are not diverted from their intended uses as sited by the users."[36] In 1971 the community entered into an agreement with the IAEA allowing the latter to verify its findings.[37]

EURATOM's inspectorate is particularly notable because it has broader authority than that of the IAEA. Its charter provides that "inspectors shall at all times have access to all places and data and equipment, or facilities."[38] Should problems arise, the community's court of justice can enforce inspection rights by issuing a warrant for this purpose. In the event of infringement of obligations, penalties in order of severity include "(a) a warning; (b) withdrawal of special advantages, such as financial or technical assistance; (c) the placing of the enterprise, for a maximum period of four months, under the administration of a person or board appointed jointly by the Commission and the State having jurisdiction over such enterprise; or (d) the complete or partial withdrawal of source materials or special fissionable materials."[39]

In 1976 another regional organization was created: the Agency for the Prohibition of Nuclear Weapons in Latin America.[40] It enforces implementation of the agreements made under the

Treaty for the Prohibition of Nuclear Weapons in Latin America, which included prohibitions against testing, use, manufacture, production, acquisition, receipt, storage, installation, deployment, and any form of possession of nuclear weapons. The IAEA oversees the agreements, and the Latin American agency supplements IAEA assessments with special reports on treaty compliance and with special inspections of its own. Any party can request an inspection to detect prohibited activity. The inspection policy includes full and free access to all places and all information, with resulting reports to be submitted to treaty parties, the United Nations, and the Organization of American States.[41] By 1981 twenty-two Latin American states were full parties to the treaty. Brazil conditionally ratified the accord, stipulating its right to explode peaceful nuclear devices, including those similar to nuclear weapons.[42] Argentina has signed but not ratified; Cuba has notably abstained from the agreement.

Bilateral safeguards and agreements for cooperation between exporters and importers are a third, less-than-global insurance. Obligations vary depending upon exporter demands. To prevent diversion of spent fuel, the Soviet Union obliges all reactor recipients to use Soviet fuel and return spent fuel rods to the USSR.[43] Canada, the United States, Australia, and Sweden require all non-nuclear-weapons importers to accept international safeguards on their entire nuclear program as a condition for cooperation. They also maintain residual rights to ensure the application of international safeguards and physical security measures. Canada also retains the right to withhold materials unless safeguards are adequately applied. Finally, Canada, Britain, Germany, and the United States individually oblige recipients to obtain their permission to retransfer items.[44]

The paucity of public information on the performance of both regional and bilateral safeguards makes evaluation difficult. Some nations have been critical of EURATOM's largely self-inspection operation.[45] There are charges that the organization has been lax in assuring the physical protection of nuclear material.[46] The Latin American agency and bilateral safeguard agreements that rely on the IAEA may not adequately compensate for suspected inadequacies. The variability in the requirements of bilateral agreements suggests that some suppliers are reluctant to bear direct responsibility for assuring that their exports are used only for peaceful purposes. However, these agreements do suggest that in most instances importers are willing to accept scrutiny of their nuclear programs beyond IAEA stipulations. Indeed, the United States was able to renegotiate many of its existing agreements under the 1978 Nuclear Non-Proliferation Act to require the application of full-scope safeguards and has cut off cooperation with countries that will not apply full safeguards.

The International Nuclear Energy Regime in Historical Perspective

Today's nuclear control structure represents three decades of difficult negotiation. It is important to remember the pulling and hauling involved in order to appreciate that, although great obstacles lie before us to improve it, comparable challenges had to be overcome to get us where we are today.

During World War II, when the United States first had to decide with which nations it would share its atomic secrets, President Franklin D. Roosevelt and Prime Minister Winston Churchill developed the Quebec Agreement of August 1943, wherein they made the first non-proliferation policy—to not communicate nuclear information to third parties.[47] With the Truman-Atlee-King Declaration of 1945, the United States moved toward internationalization of nuclear energy.[48] Elaboration came in the 1946 Baruch Plan introduced at the United Nations, which called for an International Atomic Development Authority to have "managerial control or ownership of all atomic energy activities" and "the duty of fostering the beneficial uses of atomic energy."[49]

The Baruch Plan represents the most comprehensive effort to control nuclear energy to date, but it foundered on cold war politics. The Soviets saw the plan as a guise to maintain an American atomic monopoly, if not on nuclear weapons themselves then on the functional design that could be transferred to bomb production. Further infringement of Soviet sovereignty was foreseen in the nature of the proposed International Atomic Development Authority itself, which allowed no nation the right to veto decisions.[50]

The United States soon discovered that denying nuclear energy to highly motivated nations with technological sophistication was useless. In 1949 the Soviet Union became the second member of the nuclear club, followed by Britain in 1952. Foreseeing the undisciplined spread of nuclear technology, President Eisenhower announced in December 1953 the Atoms for Peace Plan. The program called upon nations engaged in nuclear research to contribute natural uranium and fissionable materials to an International Atomic Energy Agency that would assist nations to use atomic energy for peaceful purposes such as agriculture, medicine, and electricity. Thus was conceived the centerpiece of the current nuclear regime.[51] However, its maturation was not easy. Nine difficult months of bilateral U.S.-Soviet negotiations followed. The USSR initially insisted that a ban on the use of nuclear weapons would have to precede other arrangements concerning the use or control of atomic energy, but it relented on this point in the end. The agreement in principle to create the IAEA served as a prelude to discussions over the organization's statute; more difficult negotiations followed, but by 1957, the agency was officially inaugurated.[52]

From 1957 through 1964, the IAEA was weak, with poorly articulated rules, but over time it developed an inspection system that intruded upon national sovereignty. At first, IAEA safeguards met substantial opposition from Moscow, the Soviet bloc nations, and some developing nations. The USSR repeatedly denounced the safeguards as a "spider's web, which would catch in its threads all the science and all the scientists of the world."[53] Indeed Moscow advocated another path: Soviet nuclear assistance to the world community, without strings. India also was adamantly antagonistic: "If safeguards are applied by the Agency to those states which cannot further their atomic development without the receipt of aid from the Agency or other member states, the operations of the Agency will have the effect of dividing member states into two categories, the smaller and less powerful states being subject to safeguards, while the greater powers are above them. This will increase, rather than decrease international tension."[54] The United States and its allies persisted. Roll call votes became a regular component of the debate, with the West usually winning seventeen to six in the effort to establish agency safeguards.[55]

By the time the IAEA was operational, the United States had some forty bilateral nuclear cooperative agreements for research reactors, each allowing U.S. inspection to assure peaceful use of U.S. nuclear supplies. However, many importers did not wish to accede indefinitely to U.S. inspection. With the additional personnel burden inspections placed on the United States, U.S. officials increasingly looked favorably upon the IAEA as a vehicle to enforce safeguards, which added impetus toward an agency inspectorate.[56] Although the U.S. disposition met with Soviet resistance at first, by 1959 the USSR was reevaluating its own international safeguards position, spurred by China's nuclear weapons ambitions, which the Soviets supported until they recognized the possible threat to themselves. The Soviet Union became a supporter and innovator in nuclear safeguards: Nuclear exports were limited to light water reactors that did not use weapons-grade material, all spent fuel was required to be returned to minimize the danger that importers would divert plutonium, and East European recipients were forbidden to build indigenous enrichment and plutonium reprocessing installations.[57]

The tightening of Soviet export criteria did not initially include a role for the IAEA. Thus at first, the Soviet Union, joined by its Warsaw Pact allies India and Iraq, opposed the application of safeguards for reactors producing less than 100 Mwth (megawatts thermal) and the first tripartite safeguards agreement between the IAEA, the United States, and Japan in 1963. However, Soviet opposition ended as the agency expanded its safeguards to reactors of all sizes in 1964 and to reprocessing and fuel fabrication plants in 1966 and 1968.[58] This growing IAEA responsibility was significant in overcoming the opposition of a number of Western industrial nations that were concerned that safeguards could be used for industrial intelligence. Finally, the more comprehensive set of safeguards described earlier was negotiated after the Non-Proliferation Treaty took effect.

With its new responsibilities, the IAEA expanded the number of personnel engaged in overseeing the enforcement of safeguards. In 1961 the organization had 3 inspectors; this figure

Table 2.2

Safeguards Expenditures as a Percentage of
Regular Budget and Total Budget

Year	SG Costs $1000s	Total Budg. $100s	SG as % of Total Budget
1962	253	7421	3.4
1963	385	8230	4.7
1964	334	8895	3.8
1965	354	9556	3.7
1966	417	10589	3.9
1967	483	11232	4.3
1968	596	12268	4.9
1969	953	12322	7.7
1970	1232	14093	8.7
1971	1635	17218	9.5
1972	2035	19833	10.3
1973	2564	23583	10.9
1974	3441	29273	11.8
1975	4962	35298	14.1
1976	5988	40246	14.9
1977	7701	50567	15.2
1978	12027	59035	20.4
1979	16795	75362	22.3
1980	19396	88076	23.2
1981	25003	88677	28.2
1982	29170	86369	33.7

Sources: 1962-1982, IAEA Programme and Budget Documents; 1971-1974, "IAEA Activities Under Article III of NPT," NPT/CONF/6/Rev,1,15 (April 1975); 1975-1980, NPT/CONF.II/6,2 (June 1980); Benjamin N. Schiff, International Nuclear Technology Transfer (Totowa, NJ: Rowman & Allanheld, 1984), p. 114. .

grew to 138 by 1980. In 1980 some 665 facilities were under agency safeguard and were subject to an estimated total of 1300 inspections. Supporting this endeavor was a $20 million budget representing over 23 percent of the agency's entire outlay. This was a far cry from the early days of the organization when less than 4 percent of the total expenditure was devoted to safeguards (see Table 2.2). Additionally, the IAEA developed a number of other programs to promote nuclear energy, including technical training, nuclear safety precautions, use of radiation in food preservation, and the promotion of radiation in the fields of health, the physical sciences, agriculture, and industry.[59]

It is surprising that IAEA safeguards exist at all—that nations are willing to allow extra-national entities to scrutinize what for many countries is one of the most sensitive industries is remarkable indeed. Warren Donnelly, a senior analyst of nuclear affairs with the Congressional Research Service, notes, "Safeguards are unique. It is the first time in history that sovereign states have invited an international organization to perform inspections on important installations within their territories. . . ."[60] Lawrence Scheiman, a long-time student of the growth of the international nuclear regime, makes a similar point: "The development and widespread acceptance of national commitments including on-site inspections is unprecedented in the history of the modern sovereign state."[61]

Although the international nuclear regime has made notable progress, it has also been subjected to increasing stress; so far it has withstood the strains. In 1974 India posed a major challenge by detonating a "peaceful nuclear device" that combined equipment imported from abroad with indigenous materials and plutonium produced from a Canadian-supplied reactor using heavy water from the United States. This act was disruptive, but it did not prove to be as damaging as feared. India was not a member of the Non-Proliferation Treaty, so the NPT was not violated. Since then, India has made no further detonations, nor has it expanded its resources to develop a full-fledged nuclear weapons program.

Askoh Kapur interpreted the meaning of the explosion by arguing that nations can pull back from the nuclear weapons brink: "The analogy of 'being a little pregnant' does not hold. Rather the analogy that aptly describes India's nuclear behavior is that the 'curtain can be lifted and then drawn back again.' "[62] This is not to say the event did not have its negative side effects: It clearly increased Pakistan's nuclear weapons ambitions. But it also had positive attributes—it spurred nuclear suppliers to convene talks that resulted in export guidelines by 1977.

India's test marked only the first of several nuclear proliferation brushfires in the 1970s and early 1980s. The United States acted as principal arbiter, although Canada in particular played an important role as well.[63] When Pakistan and Korea tried to acquire reprocessing plants from France, the United States acted to prevent consummation of the agreements, with apparent success.[64] In the process, the United States stimulated European sensitivity to nuclear trade as an unusual type of commerce. As one French observer, Pierre Lellouche, put it: "In retrospect, perhaps the single most important achievement of the Ford and Carter Administrations' foreign nuclear policies has been the triggering of an awareness in Europe of the fact that the exporting of nuclear material and equipment is a special business and that non-proliferation is a policy for which Europe should be responsible as well."[65]

Once alerted by the Soviets to a possible South African nuclear detonation in 1979, the United States and other governments pressured South Africa to desist.[66] However, the most dramatic effort to contain proliferation came from another source, when in June 1981 Israel destroyed Iraq's Osirak reactor, which Israel suspected was a guise for developing a nuclear weapons program. This action in turn stimulated interest in the vulnerability of nuclear plants to military bombardment, compelling the United Nations Committee on Disarmament to consider the implications more intensely. The bombing also induced greater politization of the regime from another perspective: In 1982 Israel was illegally denied credentials to attend the IAEA's annual meeting of the General Conference. The United States responded by boycotting the meeting and suspending its support for the agency. Although the matter of Israeli participation in the IAEA was resolved within a few months, which permitted U.S. recommitment to the IAEA, it raised questions about the ability of the agency to deal with external strains upon the nuclear regime. These events came on top of suspicions that Pakistan was developing nuclear weapons, the failure of the Committee on Disarmament to make progress toward banning attacks on nuclear plants, and the less than overwhelming success of the non-proliferation review conferences.

In keeping with the NPT, parties meet every five years to reassess the agreement; review conferences were held in 1975 and 1980 and one will take place in 1985. In 1975 at the NPT review conference, although consensus was reached on a final communique in support of the NPT, the superpowers were strongly chastised by other states for failing to make substantial progress in their bilateral arms control efforts, which were part of the quid pro quo for others to join the NPT.[67] The 1980 review conference was less successful for member nations: The conferees were unable to reach an accord on a final communique. Still, they came close. A final draft statement acknowledged that the NPT plays a vital role; that nuclear cooperation that contributes to development of nuclear weapons of non-NPT parties should be avoided; that continued improvements of safeguards are desirable; that convention on the physical protection of nuclear material should be adhered to; that suppliers should act reliably; that efforts should go forward toward international plutonium storage and management of spent fuel; that nuclear free zones are desirable; and that international agreements should be negotiated against the use of nuclear weapons on non-nuclear weapons states. There was stubborn disagreement over superpower progress in arms control; the supply of nuclear technology to states that failed to apply full scope safeguards; critiques of nuclear programs in Israel, South Africa, and South Asia; and veiled criticism of the United States for failing to properly secure nuclear material (presumably referring to an alleged diversion of nuclear material in Pennsylvania by Israeli agents).[68]

While the nuclear regime was being challenged, a jolt of a different sort occurred in 1979 at Three Mile Island, the most serious nuclear accident to date. Although no lives were lost, the event pointed out the fragility of nuclear facilities that, if mismanaged, could result in a life-threatening event. In the United States, Three Mile Island accelerated cynicism about nuclear power's value. Cancellation of orders for power plants in planning and construction phases occurred as the costs of new regulatory requirements generated by the accident, plus unfavorable capital markets, slow growth in electricity demand, and a lack of public confidence, led to a dramatic downturn in construction.

Despite the buffeting of the nuclear regime, long-term efforts to promote its reinforcement continued. By the early 1980s a program begun in 1974 to establish internationally agreed upon safety standards neared fruition.[69] An IAEA Committee on Assurances of Supply (CAS) was established in 1980.[70] It was an offspring of the 1977–1980 INFCE that, while considering the security problems associated with proliferation, also devoted attention to supply assurances. The CAS, which continues to meet at the time of this writing, involves over forty nations attempting to grapple with such matters as the insulation of consumers from supply interruptions and the sanctity of contracts. As of fall 1983, modest steps had been taken toward formulating general principles of cooperation, but no final report had been made.

On other fronts, there were still more positive signs. As mentioned earlier, the agency, through the late 1970s and early 1980s, steadily expanded the number of safeguard agreements consistent with the requirements of the NPT.[71] In 1975 the agency's director general inaugurated a Standing Advisory Group on Safeguards Implementation, a group of technical experts who were to study and evaluate the organization's performance. In 1977 the first Safeguards Implementation Report was completed, providing aggregate statistics and summaries to member states and a separate confidential report for top agency personnel and the board of governors, bearing on each safeguarded state.[72] On another front, the Convention on the Physical Protection of Nuclear Materials was opened for signing in 1979, providing guidelines for the physical protection of nuclear material in transit and for cooperation among parties for recovery and return of stolen nuclear material, as well as sanctions for perpetrators of such acts.[73] In 1982, the agency announced formation of the Operational Safety Review Team (OSART), which is to provide experts for any country desiring an independent assessment of the safety of its plants.[74] And, in 1984, the IAEA moved toward formation of an International Nuclear Safety Advisory Group composed of technical experts who would identify issues important to public safety.[75]

At this time the regime is battered but still viable. Evaluating it from a proliferation point of view, Warren Donnelly found several sustaining factors: (1) there has been a de facto freeze on the number of nuclear weapons states; (2) thus far, no terrorists have successfully misused nuclear power; (3) there has been a slowdown in the market for nuclear power; (4) there has been diminished use of highly enriched uranium; (5) suppliers continue to restrain themselves; (6) there is a general continued predisposition against nuclear weapons; (7) there has been an improvement in safeguards technologies. However, the regime is challenged by (1) continued wars; (2) tensions between the great powers and others; (3) doubts about security assurances; (4) holdouts from no-nuclear-weapons pledges, including notably Argentina, Brazil, India, Israel, Pakistan, and South Africa; (5) an absence of progress in nuclear disarmament; (6) continued development of nuclear power technologies; (7) further spread of sensitive technologies; (8) the existence of unsafeguarded facilities; (9) politization of the IAEA; and (10) a changing definition of proliferation. Donnelly concluded, "It appears . . . that the balance of forces opposing the regime is rather greater than the balance sustaining it."[76]

I tend to be more optimistic than Donnelly. There has always been doubt about overcoming the obstacles: In the 1950s few thought the regime would get off the ground; in the 1960s few thought that safeguards would be implementable in a world of sovereign nations. Yet, the regime has made remarkable progress. To be sure it has been strained in recent years, but I believe there is enough common interest to sustain it. No nation wishes to see a major nuclear accident; no nation wishes to experience the results of the use of nuclear weapons on its territory; and no nation wishes subnational sabotage or wartime destruction of its plants. These common interests stimulated the regime's growth in the first place—continued efforts can strengthen it in the future. Save for the phasing out of nuclear energy, which is a debatable proposition, there are few other options. Risks will always be with us, but they can be minimized. More authoritative institutions are required to apply preventive medicine to meet growing nuclear challenges.

3
Precedents and Lessons for an International Nuclear Review

The concept of an institution to anticipate technological risk and apply preventive medicine is not new. We will look at the performance of eight such institutions in this chapter, including the Nuclear Non-Proliferation Act (NNPA) of 1978, three U.S. government organizations—the NRC, ERDA, and the Arms Control and Disarmament Agency (ACDA)—as well as four international bodies—EURATOM, the Consultative Committee, the World Bank, and the IAEA. The chapter will close with theoretical reflections by noted scholars on the issue of national compliance with an international public authority.

Nuclear Regulatory Commission

U.S. nuclear regulatory policy has evolved rapidly over the last several years. The 1974 Energy Reorganization Act abolished the Atomic Energy Commission and divided its functions between two new agencies: the NRC, responsible for regulating nuclear energy including export licensing; and ERDA, a promotional institution. In 1976 an executive order refined export licensing responsibilities, and in 1977 ERDA's responsibilities were transferred to the new Department of Energy, which was established early in the Carter administration. Congress passed the Nuclear Non-Proliferation Act in 1978, which further defined U.S. nuclear export policy. For illustrative purposes we will examine the NRC's performance between 1974 and 1976.

According to the 1954 Atomic Energy Act—the foundation upon which all subsequent legislation has been constructed—before nuclear material or facilities may be licensed for export, the recipient must have an Agreement for Cooperation. The agreement was to be a statement of principles containing the terms, conditions, duration, nature, and scope of cooperation; U.S. safeguard rights; the recipient's declaration that nuclear material and facilities would not be used for research or development of nuclear weapons or for any other military purposes; and stipulations establishing when the recipient could transfer material.[1] From 1974 through 1976, agreements were negotiated by ERDA with the participation of the Department of State, approved by the president, and submitted to the Joint Committee on Atomic Energy for a stated time before taking effect. The following "major" criteria were used: the consistency of a relationship with U.S. legal and policy requirements and with other agreements, the reasonableness of the scope of the desired cooperation, the availability of comparable assistance from other countries, national security implications, and the recipient's status with respect to the NPT and IAEA obligations.[2]

Once an agreement was concluded, consummation of specific transactions required an NRC license granted on the basis of assurances that the transaction was consistent with U.S. security. To establish this consistency, the commission submitted license applications to the executive branch for advice. The State Department, acting as lead agency, consulted with ERDA, the Department of Defense, the ACDA, and the Department of Commerce to arrive at an evaluation. The following prescribed criteria had to be considered:

(1) The purpose of the export, (2) whether the export is covered by an agreement for cooperation, (3) whether the importing country has accepted and implemented acceptable international safeguards, (4) the adequacy of the importing country's accounting and inspection procedures and physical security arrangements to deal with threats of diversion of significant quantities of nuclear materials, (5) the importing country's position on non-proliferation of nuclear weapons, and (6) the importing country's understanding with the United States re-

garding the prohibition against using U.S. supplied material in the development of nuclear explosives.[3]

The Department of State was to be responsible for detailing the findings in a report to be submitted to the NRC.

The confidentiality of parts of the licensing procedure makes an assessment of it difficult. Nonetheless, the available evidence suggests that during 1974–1976, NRC approval of exports was given as a matter of course. A General Accounting Office (GAO) report found that between 1975 and January 1976, forty of forty-nine applications were accepted, and the remainder were likely to be approved because the NRC had never disapproved a license under these procedures.[4] The GAO presented evidence that the success rate reflected less the merits of applicants than NRC deference to a higher authority. Summing up its findings, the GAO noted,

> NRC officials have stated that there would probably be few cases where the Commission's judgment, in issuing an export license, would differ from that of the Executive Branch. Should there be a difference at the end of the export license review process after all exchanges between NRC and the Executive Branch, NRC officials believe that they have the final decision-making responsibility on whether to issue a license. However, NRC believes that because most export license transactions fall within the framework of agreements for cooperation developed by the Executive Branch with Congressional review and because the President is responsible for conducting foreign policy, his views on national security and foreign policy should be given great weight by NRC in making its export licensing decisions.[5]

This conclusion suggests that regulatory bodies that subordinate themselves to a higher authority that does not have coinciding interests simply cannot fulfill their mandate.

Energy Research and Development Administration

In 1976 ERDA, in collaboration with the Department of State, the NRC, and the Export-Import Bank, published a statement assessing "the environmental, social, technological, national security, foreign policy, and economic benefits and costs to the United States associated with a continuation of nuclear power export activities through year 2000."[6] The report also examined the costs and benefits of alternatives. The statement was issued in accordance with procedures and guidelines established by the National Environmental Policy Act of 1979, which mandates that the federal government anticipate and propose alternatives to acts that degrade the environment. Its purpose was "to assist government decision-makers, industry, and the public in making informed judgments on the proper nature, scope, and direction of the United States nuclear export activities, now and in the future, and the appropriate conditions that should govern those activities."[7] The statement is interesting because of the way it assessed U.S. nuclear policy and because it demonstrated the limitations of unilateral undertakings of this sort.

According to the authors, "nuclear power export activities have yielded numerous and significant benefits to the U.S. in such areas as national security, energy trade, and employment."[8] From the security and foreign policy viewpoint nuclear exports provided U.S. leverage over the global market's development consistent with the objectives of the NPT. They helped allies reduce their dependence on fossil fuels from unreliable producers and contributed to the prosperity of all countries, including developing states. Economic benefits for the United States included $1.5 billion per annum from facility and fuel exports, and a strong domestic nuclear industry.[9]

While making this case, the ERDA statement did not deny actual and potential costs. These included environmental costs from mining, land use for fabrication facilities, and waste disposal and possible security costs should materials be diverted for weapons by foreign governments or subnational groups. The statement also admitted that sabotage of facilities and materials was conceivable. However, the authors stressed that there were limitations on the United States' capacity to unilaterally diminish these costs. Physical environmental impacts abroad were beyond the analysts' resources and authority. Furthermore, any attempts could "create risks of international repercussions arising from claims of encroachment by the U.S. on other nations' sovereignty since decisions as to the acceptability of risks to health and safety of a nation's citizens and to the physical environment traditionally have been reserved to the responsible sovereign government."[10] As a remedy, the authors suggested an international assessment: "Such an international assessment would not be constrained by sovereignty problems and could prove to be a useful tool in solving the worldwide issues related to the nuclear option."[11]

Nuclear Non-Proliferation Act of 1978

Notwithstanding ERDA's reservations about the limits of unilateral assessments and the means of minimizing nuclear risks abroad, U.S. legislation embodied in the NNPA of 1978, a particularly stringent, singular effort, all but ignored this factor.[12] The act immediately cuts off nuclear benefits to states that will not meet all of its criteria, regardless of the existence of a valid agreement for nuclear cooperation. It also requires renegotiation of all agreements for cooperation to make importers conform to the following principles: (1) all exported nuclear items will be safeguarded; (2) IAEA safeguards must extend to all non-nuclear-weapons states' nuclear installations (i.e., full-scope safeguards); (3) U.S. exports will not be used for fabrication of nuclear explosive devices; (4) explosion of such devices will result in the return of all U.S. nuclear exports; (5) U.S. exports will not be transferred without U.S. approval; (6) the importer will guarantee physical security of transferred nuclear material; (7) the importer will not reprocess, enrich, or otherwise alter nuclear material derived from U.S. commerce without the approval of the United States; (8) weapons-grade material derived from U.S. commerce will be stored in facilities approved by the United States; and (9) special nuclear materials and facilities constructed or produced through U.S. transfer of sensitive nuclear technology will be subject to the above considerations. The act provides for congressional review of agreements prior to consummation and presidential discretion to grant exemptions with the approval of Congress in circumstances where U.S. nonproliferation interests are enhanced, consistent with national security.

Beyond establishing detailed U.S. export criteria, the act calls upon the executive branch to make every effort to establish greater international collaboration to minimize nuclear risks. In particular, it advocates strengthening the IAEA; developing international sanctions for violations of peaceful uses of nuclear energy; establishing international procedures to respond to diversion, theft, or sabotage; and creating international spent fuel repositories and fuel banks. To alleviate strains on fuel supply it mandates expanding the low enriched fuel capacity of the United States to help meet the world's needs.

Now that several years have passed, some judgment can be made about the effectiveness of the legislation. The act seems to have engendered resentment among some of the nations forced to rely on the United States because of its requirement that the agreements for cooperation be renegotiated. This resentment is underlaid in Europe by a feeling that the United States is attempting to unilaterally legislate for others.[13] Furthermore, both the rigor of the legislation and the complex decision-making required for an export license have raised concern about U.S. reliability as a nuclear supplier. Given less rigorous requirements of some other exporters, plus their large production reserve not only in equipment but, in the 1980s, in Europe's fuel services as well, importers increasingly will be able to avail themselves of less demanding alternatives.[14] Indeed, in 1981 the GAO concluded that the United States may have been less competitive as a result of the relatively rigorous requirements of the NNPA.[15] These considerations underscore the limitations of unilateral initiatives to control nuclear development worldwide.

Arms Control and Disarmament Agency

The U.S. ACDA is responsible for two relevant assessments. First, as part of its review process, ACDA advises the State Department on security implications arising from nuclear exports. Second, ACDA assesses the arms control implications of new weapons systems.

ACDA's Nuclear Export Review

Although the executive branch's nuclear export assessments are confidential, congressional testimony on the U.S. decision to export reactors to Egypt and Israel provided a glimpse into the workings of the ACDA in 1974. According to former ACDA Director Fred Iklé, the agency asked three questions:

> (1) Will the country that is to receive nuclear technology from the United States be likely to acquire such technology from other supplier nations? (2) Will the prospective technology transfer permit us to add further protective measures to the safeguards ordinarily applied, and thus permit us to take a step forward in separating the peaceful atom from the atom of war? (3) Is the region to which nuclear technology is exported free of latent or actual hostilities?[16]

Iklé testified that in ACDA's judgment, proposed sales to the Middle East were likely to occur whether or not the United States was involved. Furthermore, the United States would be more responsible than other countries in the application of safeguards. Iklé granted the region was prone to conflict. "But," he argued, "there is a countervailing consideration: the transfer of these power reactors can help strengthen United States influence in the area and thus help this administration and future administrations continue to bring peace to that area."[17]

Subsequent testimony by non-government witnesses questioned the basis of Iklé's testimony. Mason Willrich and George Quester, two prominent students of nuclear proliferation, argued that U.S. responsibility in nuclear trade was no greater than that of the Soviet Union, France, Canada, or West Germany. However, U.S. action in this respect would probably accelerate the military nuclearization of the region rather than curb it.[18] As for Iklé's argument that nuclear trade enhanced U.S. influence, Congressman Benjamin Rosenthal argued that there were less risky ways to achieve that objective.[19]

Two rationales can account for the inadequacy of Iklé's remarks: He was rationalizing a decision over which he had no control, and/or ACDA's assessment was not as thorough as it should have been. Both explanations illuminate problems posed by efforts to anticipate the security implications of nuclear energy. The first underscores the importance of independent authority: Without it, review agencies simply rubber-stamp the views of others. The second suggests the importance of honesty, thoroughness, objectivity, and initiative by those undertaking such assessments. Without such essential underpinning, assessments will not fulfill their objectives.

ACDA's Arms Control Assessments

In 1975 Congress amended the Arms Control and Disarmament Act to require the executive branch to assess the arms control implications of military appropriations requests.[20] Although the amendment did not deal with nuclear exports, its function is similar enough to alternatives I will propose that it provides a relevant case study.

The amendment stipulated that any agency preparing a legislative or budgetary proposal was to provide the director with detailed information if its proposal involved nuclear weapons or their delivery vehicles, military programs with a total program cost in excess of $250 million or an annual cost of $50 million, or any other program that the director of ACDA believed had "significant arms control, disarmament, or negotiation impact." The director was empowered to assess and analyze such programs in terms of their impact on arms control and was to submit the resulting recommendations to the National Security Council, the Office of Management and Budget, and the government agency proposing the program. Congress also had authorization to review the statements.[21]

In January of 1977 the Congressional Research Service (CRS) assessed arms control impact statements submitted to the Congress. It found the statements deficient in at least two regards. First, they were not comprehensive: Of more than 100 potential programs that could have been reviewed, the Defense Department reported on 21 and ERDA on 5. The Defense Department, without explanation, asserted that 76 programs did not have arms control impacts. However, the CRS concluded that at least half of these did have such implications.[22]

Second, and more serious, was the shallowness of the assessments. It is apparent that the defense agencies narrowly interpreted their statutory obligations. The Defense Department considered whether weapons systems violated existing arms control agreements or those currently being negotiated and examined their impact on strategic stability. The question of verification arose in only a few instances. ERDA addressed safety, security, and improved command and control of weapons systems. It did not address, but should have, each program's reduction of wartime destruction, inherent economic burdens, inhibition of armaments races, and impact on perceptions of national will and the military balance.

Several rationales account for the inadequacies of the statements. First, the CRS found three terms in the arms control legislation to be ambiguous: "program," "arms control," and "impact." The ambiguities left considerable room for interpretation and discretion by departments conducting the assessment. Second, it is unlikely that the departments responsible for weapons production were in the best position to critically judge arms control impacts. A third problem was the ACDA's lack of initiative in fulfilling its obligations. In the words of the CRS report, "It was expected when the legislation on the arms control impact statements was passed that the U.S. Arms Control and Disarmament Agency, which has an arms control mission, would have a major if not leading role in preparing the impact statements. There is no evidence that such a role has materialized."[23] To remedy these inadequacies, the CRS advocated more initiative from the ACDA and clarification of the term "impact" by requiring that agencies conducting the review answer a detailed set of questions.[24]

The Carter administration took such critiques to heart. It implemented very detailed procedures to govern the review process—the upshot was an increase in quality. Still, there were limits imposed by the fact that the ACDA was not solely responsible for the review. Rather it was subject to the interagency process that allowed groups unsympathetic to arms control, like the Defense Department, to impose consensus positions representing the lowest common denominator. This in turn diminished the ability of the document to sensitize Congress and the executive branch to the arms control implications of proposed weapons systems.[25] This review once again underscores the importance of authority as well as detailed criteria in evaluations.

European Atomic Energy Community

EURATOM and three other international institutions (which we'll look at later on) were mandated responsibility to assess the implications of nuclear energy. Under Article 103 of the EURATOM charter, members of the organization contemplating an export were obligated to submit prospective export agreements for review by the community's commission, which was to ensure that the agreement conformed to the organization's purposes. If the agreement impeded these purposes, the exporter was to be so advised. Presumably this advice would stimulate the supplier to reconsider its transaction. If reconsideration was not forthcoming, the exporter could be enjoined by the commission not to conclude the transaction until objections were removed, or the exporter might be obliged to subscribe to a ruling of EURATOM's Court of Justice.[26]

EURATOM has never been able to fulfill its obligations. Because it failed to integrate Western Europe's nuclear programs in any real way, it has never had authority to act against the wishes of its individual members. The organization goes through the exercise of reviewing exports, but it has always acted in a perfunctory role, rubber-stamping transactions.[27]

Consultative Committee

In the late 1940s, the United States initiated what eventually became the most concerted international effort to monitor exports of all sorts, nuclear power included, for security reasons. The United States tried to prevent deterioration of U.S. technological superiority over the Soviet Union by forbidding U.S. exports to the Soviet bloc and by pressuring its allies to do likewise. In 1949 the Consultative Committee (Cocom) was established to coordinate policies of the United States and six other nations— England, France, Italy, the Netherlands, Belgium, and Luxembourg. In subsequent years the organization was enlarged to include Norway, Canada, Denmark, West Germany, Portugal, Japan, Greece, and Turkey. For illustrative purposes, we will review its performance through the 1950s.[28]

Cocom divided commodities into three categories: embargoed products, quantitative regulated exports, and items to be kept under surveillance. At the height of the embargo, 1952–1955, over 50 percent of all internationally traded goods were on the lists, and nuclear materials were among the items totally embargoed. In later years the number of such items was reduced drastically, and by 1958, only 10 percent of internationally traded goods were on the lists. Nuclear power plants and materials were among the goods deleted.[29]

With the exception of monitoring computers and sophisticated military technologies, Cocom was not very successful. It did not prevent the Soviet Union from acquiring at least one sample of most embargoed items. Those items that the Soviets were unable to obtain at all or to obtain only in small quantities, they produced themselves after a relatively short delay or developed substitutes. One of the ironies of the embargo is that it may have forced members of the Soviet bloc into greater economic reliance on Moscow.

The principal reason for the embargo's failure was lack of multilateral support. Western Europeans felt that the restraints impeded their World War II recovery, which depended on exports. They also resented U.S. coercion, including threats to cut off assistance to uncooperative countries. Consequently, many countries allowed their firms to engage secretly in trade.[30]

The Cocom experience underscores the limits of such international efforts. U.S. allies had different economic stakes, and U.S. leverage was insufficient to induce cooperation. And the Soviets circumvented the embargo by finding adequate substitutes for the products they could not import.

World Bank

Of all the institutions examined here, the World Bank conducts the most successful review. The bank loans money for development projects such as electrical utilities and transportation networks. Although in at least one case, that of Italy, it financed a nuclear reactor, the bank no longer finances nuclear projects. I include the incident to illustrate an institution that successfully anticipates public policy risks.

To obtain the World Bank's financial support, a country must agree to a project appraisal. The bank approaches this review seriously. According to one source, the bank has learned through experience that in project appraisal nothing should be taken for granted and that healthy skepticism is a cardinal virtue.[31] The appraisal reviews the economic, technical, managerial, organizational, commercial, and financial aspects of each project. Economic assessments include the contribution of the project to the economy as a whole and its priority, taking into consideration scarce capital, managerial talent, and available skilled labor. Technical assessments appraise the engineering of the project—appropriateness of proposed methods and processes, adequacy of design, construction scheduling, and potential causes of delay. Managerial appraisals review the demonstrated competence of the state in other enterprises. Organizational reviews estimate the organizational and operational requirements needed to bring the project to fruition. The commercial analysis calculates whether adequate arrangements have been made for purchasing construction materials and whether the requirements for maintaining the project will be available after its completion. Finally, the financial analysis determines the soundness of the enterprise undertaking the project.[32]

On the basis of its review, the World Bank can refuse to support a project, recommend its delay until there are more propitious circumstances, recommend extensive modifications, or accept the proposal for funding. Once a loan is granted, the bank stays intimately involved in the project to assure that finances are properly and efficiently used. This supervision not only ensures success of the project but also reassures creditors, thereby keeping borrowing costs as low as possible.

For the caution and care it takes to evaluate projects, the World Bank has been given high marks by its creditors. Its effectiveness is further underscored by the fact that it has had few failures. However, the bank's performance has not been flawless. The World Bank has been criticized for not paying sufficient attention to ecological costs or to the long-term implications of ventures. But on the whole, the bank is praised for doing what it is supposed to do.[33] This success is largely attributed to its authority and its willingness to use that authority, to its rigorous review criteria, and to the fact that it deals with a monetary commodity.

IAEA Physical Security Guidelines

The International Atomic Energy Agency is responsible for fostering "peaceful" nuclear development worldwide. To insure that this development remains peaceful, the agency devised a number of measures, including a set of physical security guidelines for nuclear facilities and materials. Consummated in 1975, revised in 1977, and formulated into a convention in 1980, the guidelines recognize that although physical security is a national responsibility, the international implications of nuclear terrorism make it an issue of international concern.[34] Thus, the guidelines stipulate how states should protect nuclear facilities and materials in use, transit, and storage. The agency reinforces its recommendations by developing legal instruments of international cooperation, providing technical assistance in the form of advice and training, publishing practical guidebooks on comprehensive physical protection systems, and maintaining an information bank in the agency's library.

Although the security guidelines are purely advisory, the agency reports that they have been favorably received and used in "some" states for guidance in the preparation of national regulations. They are also referred to in the suppliers' general guidelines. Although not universally applied, they represent a benchmark that has had sufficient success to warrant a formal international convention.[35]

Theories on Compliance with International Public Authority

Some useful ideas for creating more authoritative mechanisms to assure compliance with international nuclear norms can be

Table 3.1

Unilateral or Multilateral Sanctions

---

o Termination of nuclear assistance, exports, and cooperation
o Complete or selective embargo on imports and exports
o Cutoff or reduction of bilateral economic assistance
o Slowdown or cutoff of World Bank loans
o Cutoff of U.S. Ex-Im Bank loans and comparable support
o Ban on private investment and lending
o Freeze on financial assets abroad
o Refusal to refinance outstanding debt
o Termination of airline landing rights
o Expulsion of foreign students working toward technical, scientific,
   engineering, and similar degrees as well as postdegree trainees
o Ban on provision of economic, technical, managerial, and other
   assistance
o Reassessment of alliance relationship
o Withdrawal of troops and other reductions of alliance commitment
o Termination of security ties
o Breaking of diplomatic relations and withdrawal of political support
o Embargo on arms sales or transfers
o Expulsion from appropriate international agencies

Source: Lewis A. Dunn, Controlling the Bomb: Nuclear Proliferation in the 1980's (New Haven, CT: Yale University Press, 1983), p. 108.

found in the writing of some prominent scholars. Oran Young defines a compliance mechanism as "any institution or set of institutions (formal or informal) established by a public authority for the purpose of encouraging compliance with one or more behavioral prescriptions of a compliance system."[36] Such institutions usually include incentives and disincentives, that is, carrots and sticks. I. William Zartman and Maureen R. Berman identify carrots as exchanges, side payments, compensation, and other contingent inducements. Sticks include sanctions or an explicit or implicit threat of sanctions.[37] In Table 3.1 Lewis Dunn identifies a range of possible sanctions for deterring nations from pursuing the nuclear weapons option. Clearly the nuclear energy regime already acknowledges the use of carrots and sticks. As a quid pro quo for joining the NPT, non-nuclear-weapons states are promised nuclear assistance. Failure to enforce IAEA safeguards on IAEA-supplied nuclear material can result in suspension or termination of IAEA aid.

Sanctions have been more difficult to apply than assistance. For example, India continued to receive U.S. nuclear aid despite its 1974 nuclear weapon detonation.[38] The difficulty in applying sanctions can be explained by cross pressures upon the applicant. According to Richard Bilder,

> sanctions may involve costs not only for the target nation but also for the nation or nations imposing the sanctions . . . ; sanctions, if imposed, may lead to resentment, increased intransigence, and further breach of international commitments by the target nation, rather than to compliance, making negotiated settlement more difficult . . . ; and, sanctions, if imposed, may lead to retaliatory action by the target nation, thus escalating the dispute or threatening peace.[39]

To avoid the dilemmas of sanctions, Young points to compliance mechanisms other than carrots and sticks. One is direct intervention, which has a familiar ring in the international nuclear regime where inspections and IAEA record-keeping diminish cheating. Young also identifies other more or less intrusive compliance mechanisms, including self-interest, social pressure, obligation, habit, or practice. He contends that such pressures work in highly decentralized environments like the international system.[40] The partial nuclear test ban treaty, which does not include a formal verification mechanism, is illustrative. At the same time, Stein points to the importance of greater institutionalization of compliance mechanisms in arms control where verification is not as easily accomplished as in the test ban.

> International disarmament agreements are notoriously problematic. Indeed, the decision to comply with or cheat on an arms control agreement is also a prisoners' dilemma situation in which each actor's dominant strategy is to cheat. Thus, it is not surprising that arms control agreements are highly institutionalized, for these regimes are continually concerned with compliance and policing. They must define cheating quite explicitly, insure that it be observable, and specify verification and monitoring procedures.[41]

Still, there is reluctance to institutionalize, since to do so involves, or is perceived to involve, a greater surrender of sovereignty than informal compliance mechanisms require. And at least in some efforts at regime-building outside arms control, namely, in international health, meteorology, and food standards, the more formal the institutionalization the less likely it is that the standards will be used by member parties; indeed, the preference is for flexible and voluntary procedures.[42]

Lessons

Where do the cases and theoretical literature leave us? Both suggest that no single formula exists to insure compliance with international norms among diversely motivated nations. Still, we can draw a number of generalizations about the requirements for successful international and national institutions that would anticipate and reduce the vulnerability of nuclear facilities to diversion, acts of war, terrorism, and accidents. Common interest is extremely important as a foundation for success, but it is a foundation difficult to construct. Cooperation can be forced as it is in Cocom; however, Cocom demonstrated that conflicting economic stakes ultimately undermine restrictive trade practices. In like manner, different bureaucratic and political concerns undermined the review efforts of the NRC and ACDA.

Common interests are necessary but may not be sufficient requisites for success. It is rare for national interests to coincide perfectly: Diverse forces are often present and tend to undermine accord. As Arthur Stein points out in the arms control area, given the propensity of parties to take advantage of agreements at the margins or beyond (as suggested by the Reagan administration allegations of Soviet cheating in SALT),[43] considerable organizational development is optimal. Such development requires that the institution have authority and independence to perform its functions, but in a community of sovereign nations, such authority is difficult to acquire. This is true even within a national setting where, as the experiences of the NRC and ACDA suggest, even statutory mandates may not be genuine. In only one case, that of the World Bank, does authority seem to have been exercised. But the World Bank is unique because it deals with money, a commodity readily understood and earnestly desired.

Still, authority can be enhanced and a regulatory regime's integrity better assured by a clear mandate. The consequences of ACDA's ambiguous mandate that allowed agencies conducting arms control reviews to be less thorough than they should have been underscored the importance of clarity. To be effective, the mandate must not be so broad that an institution is asked to perform the impossible, but not so narrow—such as ERDA's parochially focused impact statement—that it cannot perform its functions. The Congressional Research Service's criticism of ACDA's arms control assessments for failing to ask enough of the right questions and the success of the World Bank's strict standards suggest the importance of detailed review criteria. Likewise, the IAEA's physical security guidelines and the export guidelines of the suppliers group illustrate alternatives—albeit imperfect ones, due to their reliance on voluntary compliance— that establish international standards of behavior having a more palatable impact than unilaterally declared standards like those of the Nuclear Non-Proliferation Act of 1978. Clear mandates and normative criteria may themselves have to be reinforced. Carrots and sticks may have a role, but although carrots (rewards) are fairly easy to dispense, nations are far more reluctant to apply sticks (sanctions) when they experience cross pressures. International forums, with their diffuse membership, may be better able to deflect such pressures.

4
Possible Cures

Experience and the writings of theorists provide an empirical and theoretical foundation for defining institutions that could apply the preventive medicine necessary to the health of worldwide nuclear development. Certainly the deficiencies in current treatment suggest a compelling need, and it is a need that increasingly has been recognized by nuclear energy policy analysts. Warren Donnelly acknowledges that reinforcement of the international non-proliferation regime is necessary "lest it fall into disrepair and disrepute."

> In the absence of a well organized and predominant pressure for improved safeguards, and with some disinterested or contrary-minded member states, the Agency has to settle decisions and policies at the lowest common denominator. Without such pressure, the 1980s are likely to see continuing doubts about IAEA safeguards. Should confidence in them be undermined, the credibility of safeguards will obviously be at risk thereby threatening the non-proliferation regime itself.[1]

Several analysts have proposed formal institutions to strengthen the nuclear energy regime. Indeed, the literature is peppered with proposals that focus in the main on the threat posed by nuclear weapons proliferation. There are advocates of multinational fuel banks, international plutonium reprocessing, and spent fuel storage and supply regulation.[2] Others have taken bolder approaches. Michael Brenner calls for an organization akin to the London suppliers group but broader in representation, including third tier suppliers like China, as well as major consumers.

High on the agenda of such a group (or, were it to prove impractical, that of a more narrowly constituted group) should be the question of monitoring the traffic in nuclear materials, under whatever rules are agreed upon. It should explore the idea of establishing a nuclear fact-finding and arbitration service to investigate claims of clandestine weapons activity. Ideally, such a service would be coupled with a streamlining of IAEA procedures for setting in motion the sanctions process. Unfortunately, the divisiveness that recently has hampered the agency, accompanied by increasing sensitivity to encroachments on national sovereignty, does not make this a propitious time to advance plans for a more assertive role for the organization. The discrepancy between need and capability should elicit a redoubled commitment to an independent and tough IAEA and serious consideration of ways to get the job done outside the agency.[3]

Joseph Yager, in a Brookings Institution study, suggests a phased approach for improving the nuclear regime. He begins by calling for an international consultative forum to review nuclear energy challenges. Phases two and three include international plutonium and spent fuel storage.

By phase four, if not earlier, it might be possible to achieve a broad international consensus on the rules of trade in sensitive nuclear material, equipment, and technology. . . . The consensus on the rules of trade could eventually be committed to writing, such as the guidelines of the London nuclear suppliers' group have been. An attempt to formalize the consensus on a treaty would probably not be worth the effort and might lose the support of countries that would be willing to cooperate, but would not want to be legally bound to do so.[4]

At the same time, Yager is pessimistic as to whether the time is ripe for a more comprehensive body to administer the international nuclear regime: "In any event, negotiation of an agreement to establish such a body is not feasible today. At best, this concept must be regarded as an idea whose time has not yet come."[5]

Pierre Lellouche, a strategic analyst with the Institute Francais des Relations Internationales, anticipated the Brenner and Yager proposals. He calls for a compromise

> . . . by setting up an informal but effective mechanism of consultation among a small group of key suppliers and recipient nations. The group would allow the continuation of the work which began with INFCE and would inject a political dimension into the technical findings of the evaluation. In effect, this group would be a "multinational management mechanism" which could readily adapt—given its informal structure—to new problems and opportunities in international nuclear relations. In many respects, this mechanism would be comparable to the informal U.S.-Soviet Standing Consultative Commission which monitors the implementation of the SALT Agreements.[6]

Each of these proposals suggests a way we can go. All clearly advocate greater multilateral cooperation. But none comprehensively defines the performance criteria of multinational institutions. The content of fact finding, arbitration, and sanctions in Brenner's argument, the rules of trade in Yager's approach, and the "political dimension" in Lellouche's suggestion remain to be fleshed out. At the same time, there is a strain of pessimism that runs through these proposals regarding the international community's ability to move forward. Now is not the time, it is said, to create an overall body to administer the regime, however desirable. Still, we must ask: If not now, when? The following proposals are offered in the belief that now is the time for a broad approach. They reflect the common-sense principle that there is an advantage to cures that *mutually reinforce* compliance with international public authority.

The nuclear control regime can survive only by recognizing overlapping national interests and reinforcing those interests through institutions having authority, independence, a clear mandate, and analytical criteria that include both carrots and sticks. Any rigorous application of my proposals is problematic; accordingly, I have graded the relative strength of the various compliance mechanisms suggested.

The Foundation for a
New International Nuclear Regime

The history of the international nuclear regime and that of related national regulatory institutions suggest that the success of compliance mechanisms depends on nations recognizing their own interest in minimizing the threats posed by nuclear energy. Nations do not want nuclear accidents, nor terrorist acts, nor proliferation that will diminish their security, nor military destruction of their facilities. Since the IAEA's founding in 1957 nations have increasingly been willing to submit their nuclear industries to international inspections, to trade restraints, and to treaty limitations. The regime is far from perfect, but, notwithstanding recent buffeting, in many regards it has become more robust. Progress has never come easily, but in the end difficult negotiations involving carrots, sticks, and self-interest have proven fruitful. Building on this progression, I propose seven alternatives designated as International Nuclear Reviews (INRs) I through VII. Formal structure and increasing authority distinguish each level of the INRs. Each presumes that most countries share a common desire to minimize nuclear risks. What remains to be established is how far beyond current efforts the international community is willing to go.

Since this common concern must permeate whatever new institution is established, and given the importance of clear normative guidelines, the same mandate and assessment criteria apply to each INR. The mandate I envision requires that every reasonable effort be made within authoritative limitations to insure that international nuclear energy trade and domestic development do not violate, or contribute to the violation of, international security and tranquility. The mandate should include the following: (1) The export of installations and special nuclear material, as defined in an elaborated nuclear suppliers guideline, and domestic construction shall not result in violations of the principles of the first three articles of the Treaty on Non-Proliferation of Nuclear Weapons. Article I obligates nuclear weapons states to not assist non-nuclear-weapons states to acquire nuclear weapons or explosive devices. Article II commits each non-nuclear-weapons state to not manufacture or acquire nuclear weapons or other nuclear explosive devices and to not receive or seek assistance in the manufacture of nuclear weapons or explosive devices. Article III requires that each non-nuclear-weapons state accept safeguards as set forth in an agreement to be negotiated with the IAEA to verify fulfillment of obligations and to prevent diversion of nuclear energy from peaceful uses. Also, treaty parties are not to export material and equipment unless these items are subject to IAEA safeguards. (2) Nuclear material shall not be transferred by subnational or transnational groups for purposes other than energy production or peaceful scientific research and application. Facilities shall be protected against sabotage. (3) Nuclear facilities and material shall be protected against wartime destruction resulting in the release of radionuclides into the atmosphere, soil, or subsoil. (4) Facilities shall be built and operated in a manner that will minimize the possibility of accident.

Based on this mandate, a six-part Nuclear Security Assessment would be conducted by newly created INR institutions (to be described later on). The Nuclear Security Assessment would consist of a statement of the contemplated nuclear project, the economics involved, the importer's disposition toward nuclear proliferation, the prospective user's proneness to subnational diversion and sabotage, the facility's vulnerability to wartime destruction, and the importer's ability to build and operate a safe facility. The last four parts would also include a list of action *options*. (This proposed assessment procedure may raise questions about practicality; such questions are addressed in my conclusion at the end of the book.)

Proposed Nuclear Security Assessment

A. The Contemplated Nuclear Product

Each nuclear facility and material has different security implications. Enrichment and reprocessing facilities can be used to manufacture or divert materials for use in nuclear weapons. Natural uranium reactors produce more plutonium than do light water reactors and need not be shut down during refueling. Soviet reactors often lack containment shells designed to prevent the release of radionuclides; they also lack many emergency systems characteristic of U.S. reactors and are thus more vulnerable to sabotage and wartime bombardment. The first obligation of exporters, importers, and domestic producers is to consider the risks of each prospective nuclear item.

B. The Economics of Nuclear Energy

This portion of the assessment would sensitize nations to the economics of nuclear energy. Economics should be a major, though not the only, consideration in deciding to rely on atomic power. Given the costs involved, nations should be advised prior to construction about the following issues:

1. *Costs:* What are the projected planning, construction, and operational costs of the nuclear item? Answers to this question form the basis of the remainder of the economic assessment.
2. *Energy requirements:* What are the prospective user's immediate and long-term energy needs? Estimates will help determine whether nuclear power is the best source of electricity. Economical nuclear facilities today produce at least 600 Mwe. For many developing nations, this quantity may be beyond their requirements and/or distribution capabilities.
3. *The economics of the choice for nuclear power:* Is nuclear power economical for the potential buyer both in the short and long term, compared with other energy sources? Do its costs justify the quantity of scarce resources required—investment capital, domestic and foreign managerial talent, and skilled labor? (A World Bank question for determining whether it should support an export.)
4. *The balance-of-payments impact of the facility:* Many countries today have balance-of-payments problems and are unable to repay their debts. It is important that a nuclear import does not seriously exacerbate this problem.

5. *Managerial and organizational skills:* Does the prospective buyer have people with these skills? If not, what plans can be made to acquire them? (World Bank questions for establishing a project's worthiness.)

6. *Availability of energy backup systems:* Does the prospective buyer have additional generating capacity for periods during which a nuclear power plant might be inactive? Nuclear power plants do not operate year-round; there are periods when they must be shut down for maintenance and repair. Light water reactors must be shut down during refueling. During these periods a nation must have generating capacity from other sources.

*C. The Nuclear Status of the Importer
and the Importer's Attitude Toward Proliferation*

The attitude and actions of the governments of prospective buyers are the central concerns in determining proliferation risks and should be of concern to the exporter state as well as to other nations whose security could be affected by the importer's acquisition of an atom bomb. The following are logical questions to be answered when deciding on nuclear importers.

1. What nuclear resources, facilities, and materials does the importing state already possess? The answer to this question establishes the basis for subsequent questions.

2. Has the importing state signed and ratified the NPT or a similar regional treaty? If not, why not? The importing state's association with the NPT, either formally or, at the very least, by a statement of support for the principles of the treaty, should be a minimal requirement for approval.

3. If the importing state possesses any nuclear installations, are all of them under IAEA early detection safeguards? If not, why not? The failure of any non-nuclear-weapons state to place its facilities under international early detection safeguards is good reason to be suspicious about its motives. All civil facilities must be under such safeguards if the purposes of the NPT are to be realized. INRs would bear responsibility for assuring that states not living up to non-

proliferation principles are not rewarded with nuclear exports.

4. Has the prospective importer been diligent in applying international safeguards to other nuclear facilities already in its possession? INRs should not reward uncooperative states.

5. What statements regarding acquisition of nuclear weapons have been made by policymakers in the importer's government and by that government's opposing parties? Association with the NPT is necessary but not sufficient to establish an importer's nuclear weapons intentions. Signatories have the legal right to withdraw from NPT obligations; therefore, any public statements or acts either by an importer's government or by important opposition parties should be a basis for inquiry into a recipient's intentions.

6. What are the attitudes of other nations, particularly neighbors of the importing state, toward the importing state's acquisition of the proposed nuclear facilities? Since certain nuclear facilities and materials, such as reprocessing plants and plutonium, could be directed toward the fabrication of nuclear weapons, the views of concerned neighbors should be solicited and assessed.

There are several options for coping with proliferation risks.

1. If the importing state has not ratified the NPT or, at the very least, has not said it will accept in principle the NPT, it should not receive nuclear exports. This option applies to all importers and licensees, including exporters that import.

2. If the importing state possesses nuclear materials and facilities but has failed to apply international safeguards in a responsible manner then an INR regulatory institution should consider the following options:

   a. The IAEA or exporter should discuss the matter with the importer to identify the problem. The importing state should be advised that exports will be withheld until the importer rectifies the irregularities in its application of safeguards. Perhaps a trial period involving direct INR or IAEA supervision of nuclear items should be mandatory to insure the importer's adherence to the safety standards.

b. IAEA personnel should be assigned on a permanent basis to old and new facilities to watch for the possibility of violations of the safeguards.

c. Permissive action links (PALs) should be applied to certain sensitive nuclear facilities, for example, a lock on a nuclear installation to prevent withdrawal of material without consent of the keyholder.[7]

d. All spent fuel should be returned to fuel fabricators or international depositories.

e. If the importer must use recycled fuel, only those fuels that cannot be made easily into weapons materials (for example, fuel derived from a denatured thorium cycle or a heavily irradiated fuel) should be allowed.

f. Heavy water rectors that maximize plutonium production and from which fuel rods can be removed without reactor shutdown should be embargoed.

3. If the importing state seems bent on acquiring nuclear weapons,

a. All nuclear sales to that state should be prohibited, and other sticks, like those suggested by Lewis Dunn, should be considered—for example, termination of military and economic assistance or termination of security ties.

b. IAEA personnel should be assigned on a permanent basis to the suspect state's nuclear facilities; PALs should be applied; return of all spent fuel to fabricators or international depositories should be required; plutonium or highly enriched uranium-based fuels should not be exported to that state; heavy water reactor exports to that state should be embargoed; and reprocessing or enrichment capabilities should not be given to it.

D. Susceptibility of the Importing State to Subnational Diversion or Sabotage

Each nation faces different domestic problems. Some countries are chronically unstable and subject to violence; others are not. INRs should attempt to anticipate a nation's or region's proneness to diversion or sabotage and suggest protection where necessary. Indeed, the international community already recognizes this responsibility. According to Sigvard Eklund, director general of the IAEA,

> Physical protection against theft or unauthorized diversion of nuclear materials against sabotage of nuclear facilities by individuals or groups is acquiring growing importance. Although the responsibility for the establishment and operation of a comprehensive physical protection system for nuclear material and facilities within a state rests entirely with the Government of that State, it is not a matter of indifference to other states whether and to what extent that responsibility is being fulfilled. Physical protection therefore has become a matter of international concern and cooperation. The need for international cooperation has become evident in situations where the effectiveness of physical protection in one state depends on the taking of adequate measures also by other states to deter or defeat hostile actions against nuclear facilities and material, particularly when such materials are transported across national frontiers.[8]

INR questions about diversion and sabotage should include the following:

1. What are the prospects for civil disorder and violence in the importing state?
2. If the prospective buyer already possesses sensitive nuclear facilities, does it apply IAEA guidelines for physical protection? If not, why not? All user nations should apply minimum security standards, and in particularly vulnerable operations, they should apply more stringent measures (for example, protecting nuclear installations with military personnel).

3. How adequate is the prospective buyer's protection of nuclear material in transit? All nuclear material, and particularly plutonium and highly enriched uranium that can be transformed easily into weapons material, must be appropriately safeguarded in transit.

4. If the prospective buyer already possesses nuclear facilities, are they under international early detection safeguards? If not, why not? Has the prospective buyer been cooperative in the application of international safeguards? If not, why not? These questions are pertinent to subnational acts of diversion or sabotage as well as to proliferation: Although subnational groups might have more difficulty in diverting fissile material than would governments, it is incumbent upon all countries to prevent diversions.

5. Where does the prospective buyer plan to build a nuclear facility or store radioactive products in relation to populated areas? In relation to international borders? Successful sabotage of nuclear installations will result in the release of radioactive materials, possibly borne across international boundaries by either air or water. Therefore, INRs should consider the implications of facility location. If a facility is to be built near an international border, the proximate country or countries should be consulted.

6. Can an accurate forecast be made of the likelihood of future civil violence? What kind of violence might occur? These are two very difficult questions. There may be situations where civil disturbances, which have been chronic in the past, are likely to continue (for example, in Northern Ireland and Lebanon).

7. Does the prospective user have an adequate plan for dealing with attacks against nuclear facilities or with attempted diversions? Each user must have such a plan.

The following options describe ways to cope with subnational sabotage and diversion.

1. If the prospective buyer is susceptible to chronic violent civil disturbances, it should not be given nuclear energy technology.

2. If the prospective buyer is subject to sporadic civil violence, it should submit itself to upgraded IAEA oversight and follow agency guidelines aimed at minimizing the vulnerabilities of its nuclear installations and materials to subnational acts. Any prospective buyer in this category that refuses to accept appropriate safeguards should not be given nuclear facilities or materials.

3. If the prospective buyer does not have a history of significant civil violence, it should nonetheless apply IAEA physical security guidelines. Exports should not be made to countries that refuse to apply security guidelines.

4. If the prospective buyer has resisted or failed to apply international early detection safeguards, measures for coping with proliferation risks as outlined should be considered.

5. A prospective buyer should not transport plutonium or highly enriched uranium unless it can take adequate security measures.

6. When siting facilities, consideration should be given to the concerns of neighboring states over possible releases of radionuclides.

7. Unless the prospective buyer has adequate emergency plans, nuclear products should not be exported to it nor should it fabricate its own.

E. Wartime Vulnerability

Many nations face military threats of one kind or another. Some regions, like Latin America, experience little interstate conflict, whereas other areas, notably the Middle East, experience chronic wars. Military capabilities vary widely—some states have nuclear weapons and advanced delivery systems, others rely upon sophisticated conventional weapons, and still others have relatively unsophisticated arms. In the same way, the wartime vulnerability of nuclear facilities varies in different regions. The following list offers ways to ascertain the degree of vulnerability to which a facility is exposed. Recent events from 1945 onward can serve as historical evidence for the questions that follow.

1. What is the prospective buyer's susceptibility to war?
2. What were the causes of wartime involvement—colonial, territorial, material, or ideological? A statistical listing of wartime involvement without consideration of its roots would distort future projections.
3. Have wars taken place in the prospective buyer's territory? Many recent conflicts have arisen far from the combatants' territories, including the Korean and Vietnam wars. This question, like the preceding one, is designed to eliminate distortion arising from a statistical review of wartime involvement.
4. What issues might cause the prospective buyer's participation in a war involving its own territory? Only the involvement of the buyer's own territory should be of concern to INRs.
5. How likely is it that wars will involve nuclear weapons? For regions such as Europe, where the probability of nuclear warfare is great, nations should assess whether added radionuclides resulting from the destruction of the energy installations would be significant enough to warrant additional protective measures for nuclear plants.
6. What are the military capabilities of the prospective buyer's adversaries? Nuclear installations are most vulnerable to high explosives delivered by precision-guided munitions.
7. How much violence and discrimination in targets are likely to occur between adversaries during conflict involving the buyer's territory? Some Arab-Israeli wars and some South Asia conflicts were characterized by discriminate bombardment. Principal targets were the antagonist's armed forces rather than civilian populations and industrial centers. Discriminating warfare should be reinforced by a treaty banning the destruction of nuclear energy facilities.
8. Where are facilities to be situated in relation to population areas? The location of installations is an important factor in determining the consequences of contamination.
9. What is the status of the prospective buyer's civil defense? Casualties resulting from radioactive releases can be reduced if civil defense is adequate.

The following options may reduce wartime vulnerability of nuclear facilities.

1. Nuclear facilities should not be built in regions where war is likely.
2. Nuclear plants should be located in geographically remote areas; for countries bordering on oceans and seas, large bodies of water must be considered territory, since the seas can act as a holding tank for the deposit and dispersal of nuclear releases.
3. Underground siting of nuclear reactors and radioactive products should be considered.
4. Containment shells and other safety systems should be reinforced to better withstand conventional weapons bombardment. Civil defense should be strengthened.
5. Reactors that are inherently more resistant to radionuclide release should be considered—for example, the high temperature gas reactor or the "process inherent ultimately safe reactor" proposed by Sweden.[9]
6. Facilities should be located in the vicinity of populations or valued land if this enhances international stability through mutual vulnerability of antagonists.
7. Military defenses should be strengthened.
8. An economic assessment of each option above should be conducted.

F. Nuclear Safety

Because radiation releases can cross international boundaries, safe operation of a facility is a matter of concern to the international community. The ability of prospective buyers to build and operate nuclear installations safely should be considered by INR evaluators before states are allowed to undertake such programs.

1. If the prospective buyer already operates nuclear facilities, what is its safety record? Certainly if the prospective user has encountered operational problems, its ability to manage a new project should be investigated before it begins a

new undertaking. This principle increasingly has aided nuclear regulation in the United States.

2. Does the prospective buyer have adequate personnel to license, build, operate, and assure the safe operation of nuclear facilities and the safe disposition of nuclear products? Are there adequate licensing criteria? The buyer must have adequate personnel and licensing procedures as defined in IAEA guidelines in order to satisfactorily manage nuclear installations.

3. If the prospective buyer already operates nuclear installations, have its safety standards and methodologies been updated? Safety standards are continually modified by new findings, and facilities' procedures and practices should be kept up to date as well.

4. Has the prospective buyer considered IAEA health and safety guidelines in siting the installations or material it proposes to use? What is the distance between the installation site and populated areas? Is the facility liable to be flooded? What is the site's proximity to active earthquake faults? Can the buyer cope with siting peculiarities? Safe operation requires that each of these matters be thoroughly evaluated.

5. How competent are domestic contractors to perform their construction tasks? Construction requires engineering competence as well as building skill.

The following are the safety controls that should exist in determining an eligible buyer.

1. If the prospective buyer has a questionable safety record as defined by INR evaluators, the inadequacies should be rectified before any additional facilities are built.

2. If the prospective buyer does not have adequate personnel based on IAEA guidelines to license, build, operate, and assure the safety of nuclear facilities, it should not build facilities.

3. Unless the prospective buyer agrees to apply the most up-to-date safety standards recommended by the IAEA, it should not build facilities.

4. Exporters should provide importers with adequate safety guidance.
5. If domestic contractors are not competent as defined by INR evaluators, foreign contractors should be used for plant construction.

The following section examines how the seven INR institutions can apply the Nuclear Security Assessment.

The International Nuclear Reviews

INR I

INR I would make the least rigorous application of the Nuclear Security Assessment. Consistent with its policy of publishing guidelines on physical security and nuclear safety and its charter obligations to insure the peaceful and safe development of nuclear energy, the IAEA or a separate institution (see INR V and VI for elaboration) would simply publish the assessment and suggest that exporters, importers, and domestic producers consider it. Although there would be no enforcement, the guidelines with IAEA sanction would serve as a standard of behavior as some guidelines have in other circumstances.

INR II

In INR II the IAEA's (or a separate institution's) responsibilities would be expanded to apply the Nuclear Security Assessment to both export and domestic construction. For this purpose a standing committee of technical experts and social scientists would be established. This committee could be an elaboration of the current Standing Advisory Group on Safeguard Implementation or the International Commission on Nuclear Safety. Its task would be facilitated by access to IAEA inspectorate reports on facilities under construction and in operation. Nuclear Security Assessments could either be circulated to safeguard division personnel and/or member states privately or be published widely, although publication is likely to meet with national resistance. These assessments notwithstanding, the agency would have no control over nuclear development other than through the persuasiveness of its impartial findings, pressures interested nations might attempt to apply, and, should the reports be published, public opinion.

INR III

INR III involves only suppliers of nuclear equipment and material. The suppliers would expand and elaborate their current guidelines to incorporate those portions of the Nuclear Security Assessment which they do not now include. As they currently stand, the supplier guidelines are quite limited, focusing on control over the export of sensitive nuclear facilities and material that pose a proliferation threat; they do not prod exporters to consider the breadth of additional threats posed by nuclear energy. Furthermore, supplier guidelines are not as demanding as the proposed Nuclear Security Assessment in requiring full-scope safeguards and in scrutinizing the disposition of states to acquire nuclear weapons. As in the case of current supplier guidelines, the application of the Nuclear Security Assessment in INR III would be voluntary and would rely on the existing standard of behavior to influence exporters.

INR IV

INR IV calls for the suppliers group to establish a standing committee of technical experts and social scientists drawn from each of the suppliers to review major nuclear exports in terms of the Nuclear Security Assessment. As in the case of INR II, conclusions of the review could be circulated privately or published. Although the committee would exercise no formal authority, it would serve to sensitize exporters to problems associated with their trade.

INR V

INR V would create an authoritative Nuclear Exporters Review Board (NERB) composed of members of the suppliers group, as well as such emerging reactor component suppliers as Argentina, Brazil, China, South Korea, and India. Israel, Pakistan, South Africa, and Spain might also be included.[10] The NERB would approve all major defined nuclear exports on the basis of the Nuclear Security Assessment's mandate. Unlike the IAEA, the NERB could discriminate among nuclear recipients: Nations that act contrary to the nuclear regime would not receive assistance. To achieve this discriminating power, the NERB must be independent and capable of enforcement, lest it become a rubber stamp, as at times EURATOM, the NRC, or ACDA has appeared to be. A refused nation could not appeal to other authorities (for example, the IAEA Board of Governors or the United Nations) nor could recommendations arising from such sources be anything but advisory. The NERB would be staffed with technicians and social scientists who would prepare the Nuclear Security Assessments and recommendations for consideration by a board of governors comprised of a single representative for each exporter. The board would make decisions by consensus or by substantial majority, that is, two-thirds of the membership, the latter being consistent with voting procedures used by the IAEA Board of Governors. Failure to decide would result in deferring the export request. This provision should encourage the importer to meet objections with appropriate remedies. To diminish economic competition that might undermine cooperation among exporters or the success of the board, a market-sharing formula might be employed. Senator Abraham Ribicoff proposed such a formula, calling for

> agreed minimum sales for each supplier country, or an agreed quantitative sharing of reactor orders. Under this approach, each supplier would be guaranteed a minimum number of reactor sales a year, or a pro rata share of the capacity. Ideally, the market would be divided in such a way that each supplier would be able to sell the maximum number of reactors which it is able to produce and for which complete fuel services can be provided. If the market would not support the maximum capacity of each supplier, sales quotas would be cut back generally in proportion to each supplier's productive capacity as a percentage of the total capacity of the suppliers.[11]

Ribicoff acknowledges that the proposal must overcome some obstacles. It might be difficult to match importers with their preferred manufacturers. Quotas acceptable to all suppliers might be difficult to achieve. But, he argues, these problems can be solved. The nuclear market would be better understood and importers better matched with suppliers if reactor orders were reviewed en masse at regular intervals, perhaps quarterly, semi-annually, or annually. Arriving at an equitable quota might require some U.S. sacrifice, given U.S. domination of the market. However, the costs to U.S. firms could be alleviated by agreements allowing them to supply a greater share of components. Furthermore, as part owners of overseas concerns, or licensors, many of these firms benefit from production abroad. (In the mid-1970s, 40 percent of General Electric's nuclear revenues came from foreign sources.) This trend continues in the mid-1980s and may increase in the years to come.

Since Ribicoff's proposal, the nuclear export market has become considerably less robust. Some may argue that this decrease in the market will greatly spur intense competition, but it could also encourage exporters to cooperate so that each is assured some fraction of the export market and a better position from which to plan the future of its nuclear fabrication industry. Still, there are other obstacles, such as pricing mechanisms, auditing of transactions, entry allowances for newcomers, and enforcement mechanisms. Overcoming these obstacles may be more difficult, but not impossible.

INR VI

INR VI would involve importers in an expanded NERB, whose responsibilities would be the same as those assumed by the board under INR V, that is, assessing all exports through application of the Nuclear Security Assessment. Inclusion of importers in the decision-making process would overcome continuing criticism of the suppliers group as a secretive, unduly select institution. Since membership in such an organization would be more comprehensive than that of the Nuclear Exporters Review Board, this International Nuclear Review Board (INRB) could be a unit within the IAEA, allowing it to take advantage of the agency's resources, including reports of its inspectorate. However, since the IAEA is principally a promotional institution with a mandate "to accelerate and enlarge the contribution of atomic energy to peace, health, and prosperity throughout the world," it may be that the expanded NERB should be a totally independent body.

Assuming the NERB is an independent organization, its structure could include a General Conference, a Board of Governors, and a Secretariat. The General Conference would have a membership identical to that of the IAEA and its functions would be similar. It would meet annually or at special sessions convened by the institution's administrative officer, the general secretary, to review the performance of the organization and to make recommendations to the Board of Governors concerning the institution's powers and functions.

The locus of authority would be the Board of Governors, a representative group of exporters and importers. The board would assess the security implications of nuclear exports and anticipate and prevent violations of international security in keeping with its charter. It would review the Nuclear Security Assessments prepared by the Secretariat and would be responsible for assuring equitable division of the nuclear market and fair pricing among suppliers. Board decisions would be made by either consensus or by vote of two-thirds of the membership, the latter being consistent with voting procedures by the IAEA Board of Governors. Failure to decide would result in deferring the export request, which, again, should encourage the importer to meet objections with appropriate remedies.

The Secretariat would be under the board's aegis. Headed by a director general, the Secretariat would be divided into three working groups: the Exporters Apportioning Group, the Economic Assessment and Appeals Group, and the Security Review Group. Each body would provide the Board of Governors with necessary data. The Exporters Apportioning Group would be composed of representatives of all exporting states and would be responsible for dividing the nuclear market among the exporters in an equitable manner. The Economic Assessment and Appeals Group would be composed of international civil servant economists; it would assure that exporters adhere to fair market principles and would prepare the economic portions of a Nuclear Security Assessment. The Security Review Group

Table 4.1

International Nuclear Review Summary

INR	Composition	Structure	Authority	Enforcement Options
I	IAEA	Ad hoc committee	Promulgate Nuclear Security Assessment	Informal: self-enforcement and peer pressure
II	IAEA	Standing social science and technical expert group	Monitory application of Nuclear Security Assessment	Informal: self-enforcement and peer pressure
III	Current and emerging nuclear suppliers	Ad hoc committee	Promulgate Nuclear Security Assessment	Informal: self-enforcement and peer pressure
IV	Current and emerging nuclear suppliers	Standing social science and technical expert group	Monitory application of Nuclear Security Assessment	Informal: self-enforcement and peer pressure
V	Current and emerging nuclear suppliers and importers	Nuclear Export Review Board (NERB): standing social science and technical expert group; Board of Governors	Mandatory application of Nuclear Security Assessment	Applies to INR V, VI, and VII: modify user's behavior via discussions; threaten to withhold nuclear assistance; withhold nuclear assistance; IAEA personnel employed permanently to monitor nuclear facilities; apply permissive action links; limit use of plutonium and highly enriched uranium; return spent fuel to supplier or international repository; limit use of heavy-water reactors; threaten political and economic sanctions; apply economic and political sanctions.
VI	Current and emerging nuclear suppliers	International Nuclear Export Review Board (INERB): standing social science and technical expert group; Board of Governors, Secretariat; Director General; General Conference	Mandatory application of Nuclear Security Assessment	
VII	Current and emerging nuclear suppliers and importers	International Licensing Board	Mandatory licensing of all nuclear facilities worldwide	

would be composed of international civil service social scientists and technical experts who would determine security implications of nuclear exports, making assessments on the basis of the Nuclear Security Assessment.

INR VII

INR VII would require IAEA licensing of all nuclear facilities, whether imported or domestically produced. A licensing board similar to the board of governors and its support staff in INR VI would be established, which would apply a common standard of behavior to all nuclear construction and operation worldwide. No nuclear facility could operate without its sanction. In essence, the licensing board would operate as the U.S. Nuclear Regulatory Commission is supposed to operate. Table 4.1 summarizes and compares each INR alternative in terms of composition of the membership, organizational structure, authority, and enforcement options.

5
Relative Merits of the International Nuclear Reviews

Each of the INRs can be evaluated by various criteria, but certainly desirability and attainability are among the most important. Desirability is measured in terms of relative benefits compared to current protective measures and proposed alternatives. Certainly all of the INRs are more comprehensive and most are more authoritative than institutions addressing nuclear risks today. Of course, the INRs are not the only course of action, as mentioned earlier. Multinational fuel cycle centers and fuel banks have been suggested to eliminate the necessity for national enrichment and reprocessing facilities that are sources of weapons materials. Also, proposals for reducing incentives for national proliferation, including enhancing the security of states through conventional weapons sales, strengthening alliances, issuing a no-first-use declaration by nuclear armed states, and establishing new nuclear free zones, have been put forward.[1] The International Nuclear Fuel Cycle Evaluation Conference attacked the problems of national and subnational diversion from another angle. It tried to devise alternate fuel cycles from which material diversion would be difficult. Regarding wartime vulnerability, I proposed earlier a treaty that would prohibit both the threatened and actual destruction of all nuclear facilities.[2] Another panacea, proposed by David Lilienthal, is a unilateral U.S. embargo on nuclear exports.[3]

The INRs do not necessarily exclude these proposals: In some instances, the INRs complement them. Certainly multinational fuel centers should be subject to a security review suggested by the Nuclear Security Assessment. A treaty prohibiting destruction of nuclear installations in war reinforces INR efforts in safeguarding large fuel centers. The INRs would apply Lilienthal's embargo on a selective basis with international legitimacy. Finally, the INRs offer an alternative to security-strengthening measures that in some instances—for example, conventional arms transfers that could instigate an arms race or alliance obligations that countries are not prepared to assume—may be unacceptable or unachievable prescriptions. INRs provide a comprehensive approach to nuclear risks, complementing the best proposals.

There is yet another important question: Are INRs, however authoritatively applied, a good idea or do they rest on dubious assumptions with inherent flaws? To assume the INRs are worthwhile suggests first that the problems they treat are worth treating. To believe otherwise, one would have to feel that the risks I have discussed are overdrawn, that proliferation of nuclear weapons has not in the past destabilized international politics nor is it likely to do so in the future; that subnational diversion of nuclear materials and sabotage are difficult and are inconsistent with terrorist aims and therefore are not likely to occur. (The destruction of nuclear facilities resulting in a major release of radioactive products is not consistent with Clausewitz's dictum that war is the pursuit of politics.)[4] Finally, many believe the probability of a significant accident is very low. In several cases the INRs could be criticized for creating bureaucracies in a field where safeguards are alleged to be already sufficient, thereby impeding nuclear development.

In my opinion, this train of thought is overly sanguine about the problems posed by nuclear energy when the application of preventative medicine would not exact inordinate costs. In making this judgment, I accept that the risks elaborated at the beginning of this study are serious and realistic. International politics probably would be more complicated and dangerous if more states acquired nuclear weapons. Although subnational diversion and sabotage are difficult, there should be international standards to assure that they remain so in this age of growing public technological expertise. There *is* sufficient precedent to support the proposition that nuclear facilities might be attractive targets in time of war, and the low accident probability should be kept low by ensuring that states operate their facilities safely.

A more serious criticism of the INRs might be that they could not be successful for two main reasons. First, the proposals rely on the dubious assumption that by preventing nations from acquiring nuclear energy or by careful regulation of facilities, INRs will also prevent them from acquiring nuclear weapons or induce them to guard what they have more carefully against subnational diversion, sabotage, acts of war, and accident. Second, the INRs' capabilities are based on the ability to forecast future events—portions of the Nuclear Security Assessment demand projections about the importer's attitudes toward the acquisition of nuclear weapons, its susceptibility to civil disorder that might result in nuclear sabotage or diversion, and the likelihood of wartime violence in its territory.

The first criticism has already been applied to the nuclear energy proliferation nexus. According to the argument, stopping a nation from acquiring nuclear energy will not stop it from building an atom bomb. If a nation wants a weapon, the energy facility route is not the best way to obtain one; construction of facilities to produce weapons material is the most direct path. However, Albert Wohlstetter, who has reviewed the above proposition, asserts that civil energy plants do provide a nation with the weapons option.[5]

Wohlstetter contends that acquiring weapons material through the civil energy route is less costly economically, temporally, and politically. If one has acquired nuclear facilities or material for overtly civilian purposes, the "extra" costs incurred by the decision to acquire nuclear weapons "is anywhere from one to five orders of magnitude lower than the route by way of totally dedicated facilities—*not*, as one might infer if one considered total rather than incremental costs, one or two orders of magnitude higher" (emphasis included).[6] The temporal and political benefits lie in the fact that "civilian cover reduces the interval between what is overtly civilian and what is unambiguously military."[7] These propositions are all the more significant because a civilian route to nuclear weapons has been more commonplace than is usually appreciated.

Three of the last four countries to make and test nuclear explosives—that is, the three in which the evidence is public: the United Kingdom, France, and India—decided to produce and separate plutonium well before they overtly decided on a nuclear explosives program. The decision to get plutonium carried these governments along most of the path toward a bomb, but left it ambiguous as to just where the path would end. The ambiguity may, at the early stages, have reflected some uncertainties and indecision in the governments themselves, or it may, in the later stages in particular, have been ambiguous only so far as the public is concerned.[8]

The logic of Wohlstetter's argument suggests that one of the consequences of the INRs' activity might be to induce states to manufacture their own civil nuclear facilities, rather than import them, as the guise for a weapons program. However, this consequence, at least for the forseeable future, is unlikely. Most states, including many industrial countries, must rely on some imports for their nuclear industry. Although information about nuclear energy is widely disseminated, it is one thing to build small, experimental plants and quite another to build commercial installations and the parts to maintain their operation. Because of the reliance of most states on imports, some INR procedures might be able to exercise leverage not only in controlling proliferation, but also in controlling other risks.

At the same time, it must be acknowledged that at least with regard to controlling proliferation the INRs will be more successfully applied to some classes of nations than others. As Stephen M. Meyer of MIT points out, middle-core proliferants such as South Korea and Taiwan for which political, military, and economic costs of going nuclear might not be worth the price and such soft-core proliferants as Sweden or Switzerland, which have advanced technical capabilities but low incentives, will be more easily treatable under the INR-like controls than hard-core proliferants. Meyer includes in this last group Pakistan, Iraq, and Libya. Israel and South Africa could be added.[9] Although Meyer contends such nations are unlikely to be treatable through technological control, he may overstate the case. Clearly Israel and South Africa are not treatable. Perhaps not even Pakistan, although one can envision or hope for a nuclear weapons free zone in the region where international controls play an important role. By contrast, technical controls and safeguards over nuclear development in Iraq and Libya still can be effective if applied thoroughly. Certainly business as usual will not encourage respect for international norms.

The second criticism is also hard to dispute: There is no question that any attempt to forecast political upheavals will be difficult. Difficulties arise when assessments are made on the basis of a country's disposition and past actions, for situations can change rapidly. The inherent problems of accurately forecasting unrest may be the most serious charge that could be made against the INRs. However, forecasters generally *can* make gross two-to-three-year projections, and perhaps beyond, about the stability of regions and countries. Through their review, they might also uncover reasons for precautionary measures that may not be overtly apparent. One obvious region where problems are likely is the Middle East. Congressional testimony cited in Chapter 3 established that, despite the fact that the region is chronically war torn, when the United States planned to export nuclear power plants to Egypt and Israel, it barely considered the vulnerability of the facilities and the consequences of a bombing. A thorough assessment procedure would necessitate consideration of these factors. Furthermore, in cases where the character of a nation changes rapidly, for example Iran, the international community should have a common means of addressing new challenges. Through their review procedures the proposed INRs provide such a means.

Are INRs consistent with the "inalienable right" granted signatories of the NPT to research, produce, and use nuclear energy for peaceful purposes? INRs would make demands on states that may not have been made in the past, but these additional demands would not preclude peaceful uses of nuclear energy. Each nuclear control organization or codification requires that states agree to greater scrutiny to make the world increasingly safer. Each was created because existing institutions were inadequate. The INRs would further progress toward world safety.

Importers may object that some INRs make demands of them not made of exporters or of nations that fabricate their own

installations or materials. However, many exporters are themselves importers of some nuclear technologies and would therefore fall under INR scrutiny. Furthermore, exporters are already
sensitive to most security risks (the major exception being
wartime vulnerability) and are endeavoring to minimize them.
One also might argue that nations subject to sanctions will
develop entirely indigenous nuclear industries so as to break
their dependence on others. This is unlikely, save for the major
nuclear manufacturers, given the complexity and capital costs
involved. Even advanced industrial countries like Belgium and
England today import 25 percent of their nuclear hardware.[10]

Yet another argument against the INRs is that their application
would be so rigorous as to stop most nuclear trade and cooperation. Those who would make this charge must consider what
harm unbridled development could do to international well-
being. The purpose of the alternatives I have presented is not
to prevent nuclear development but to insure that it progresses
in accord with common international norms. Is a standardized
Nuclear Security Assessment really necessary? Perhaps the views
of Morris Rosen, director of the IAEA's Division of Nuclear
Safety, best explain why strong international standards are in
the best interest of all nations.

> International cooperation has contributed, through standards
> development and information exchange, to a high safety level
> in the design and operation of nuclear installations world-wide.
> Thus, the idea of also developing an international agreed-upon,
> overall concept for nuclear safety merits consideration. National
> approaches to nuclear safety developed over the years have
> resulted not only in differences in relations, but also in variations
> in technical requirements from one country to another. This has
> been a burden of the international nuclear market, and it has
> possibly had an effect on the level of public confidence. The
> development of a clear and universally acceptable approach to
> safety guided by an international body composed of prominent
> exporters might well alleviate national and international safety
> concerns, and might also positively influence public opinion.[11]

Clearly Rosen's proposal is consistent with my Nuclear Security
Assessment and some INRs. It suggests that, at least in the

mind of one prominent international nuclear civil servant, standardized reviews may help overcome politics that characterize international institutions.

Assuming the merits of the Nuclear Security Assessment and INRs, can they be established? How far is the international community likely to go to increase security? Are nations likely to give up more of their sovereignty? Former Nuclear Regulatory Commissioner Victor Gilinsky says, "Probably not, but one hopes that nations will agree to give up more of their sovereignty than they have in the past. It is clear that nuclear technology and unlimited national sovereignty are just not compatible if we want to keep from blowing ourselves up."[12] Whether Gilinsky's hope can be translated into fact can be determined only by a resolute test of international will. A conference of all current and prospective users of nuclear energy should be convened and/or a resolute effort made by the nuclear suppliers group to apply the Nuclear Security Assessment. Would nations attend? Would they agree? Some thought the International Nuclear Fuel Cycle Evaluation could not be convened; yet, nations found it in their interest to attend. The scope of the conference I suggest goes far beyond that of INFCE, which focused on technical matters, but this breadth can serve as an incentive to resolve many troubling issues now clouding the safe, peaceful development of nuclear energy.

One cannot predict the outcome with certainty, but it is reasonable to expect that some INR alternatives will be easier to attain than others. Because INRs I and III simply require circulation or publication of Nuclear Security Assessments by the IAEA and the nuclear suppliers group, respectively, without authoritative application and are consistent with the accepted practice of published guidelines, they would appear to be the easiest to achieve. They also provide the foundation for more authoritative actions. Of the two, INR III is likely to be more attainable because there is greater consensus among exporters; still, IAEA sanction, representing the cross section of nuclear users, would be desirable. Even more desirable, because they exact a stricter standard of conduct, are the remaining INRs. They will be difficult to attain because nations dislike international scrutiny of their affairs, but negotiations might focus immediately on these bolder initiatives to test how much progress could be made.

The willingness of many states to submit to IAEA inspection and the application of early detection safeguards suggest that hard bargaining can achieve significant results. At the same time, it must be acknowledged that bringing a large number of nations into a formal conference setting is cumbersome and time consuming: It is often uncertain that consensus can be built.[13] Therefore, a search is warranted for alternative strategies to stimulate international interest in INRs. Given the vanguard role the United States has usually taken in the non-proliferation arena, Washington should make low-key efforts on a country-by-country basis to build the desired consensus toward an INR consensus.[14] A formal conference can then be convened to ratify the results.

Given the risks posed by nuclear energy and the deficiencies of current methods for minimizing them, I hope that this discussion will stimulate serious thought about the INRs and their usefulness. The INRs provide a means of averting sub-national diversions, sabotage, and serious accidents. They could diminish the consequences of wartime actions against nuclear facilities. They could also halt or slow nuclear weapons proliferation. Efforts of this sort are not cost-free. Nations would have to agree to greater international scrutiny of their nuclear programs, but this cost is nominal compared to the consequences of a nuclear incident. Preventive medicine will be far more effective than post-incident cures; we cannot afford to catch the "diseases" that unregulated development may unleash. The INRs take advantage of a proven and increasing disposition of countries to reduce the risks of nuclear energy through international institutions and go beyond current efforts to comprehensively and authoritatively treat the problems—before it's too late.

6
Epilogue: The Implications
of the 1985 NPT Review Conference

As this book was published, parties to the Non-Proliferation Treaty met in Geneva in August and September 1985 for the third conference to monitor the treaty's performance, as mandated by the accord. The gathering represented a pivotal test of one foundation of this book, namely the ability of the nuclear energy regime to support further strengthening.

Prior to the meeting the outlook did not seem promising. I noted on page 48 Warren Donnelly's admonition that "forces opposing the regime appear greater than those sustaining it." This judgment was echoed forcefully by William Epstein, a long-time student of non-proliferation and currently senior special fellow with the United Nations Institute for Training and Research, and Paul Leventhal, president of the Nuclear Control Institute in Washington, D.C., just prior to the review conference.[1] Reflecting the views of a number of diplomats and arms control specialists, both painted an ominous picture. Recalling the failure of the 1980 review conference to arrive at a final declaration, coupled with the continuing inability of the superpowers to live up to their NPT Article VI obligations to pursue nuclear arms control in good faith, Epstein forecast, "The outlook for this year's conference is bleak or bleaker. The frustration of the neutral and non-aligned countries appears to be turning into resentment and anger because they believe the nuclear powers have misled them."[2] Both Epstein and Leventhal foresaw walk-outs from the conference and possible withdrawals from the NPT itself. The only optimistic scenario in Epstein's mind was one where "the Western nations would continue their previous reliance on 'damage limitation' strategy wherein they would try to prevent defections from the NPT. Perhaps the best they can hope for is that the debates of the conference will end, as in 1980, without adopting any final declaration."[3] In a more pessimistic vein Leventhal contended that notwithstanding the feverish efforts of the United States, the Soviet Union, and Britain in a damage limitation effort to save the parley, "the treaty and its review conference risk becoming irrelevant to the very arms control problems that they intended to address and prevent."[4]

With these negative prognostications, it came as a surprise that the review conference achieved the inconceivable—a consensual final resolution demonstrating that the nuclear regime is far more vigorous than many people heretofore believed.[5] Indeed, delegates report that while there were difficult negotiations, there was widespread goodwill toward the treaty and the underlying nuclear regime.[6] What is even more heartening from the perspective of this book is that the final resolution addressed each of the security risks discussed herein, supporting in every case greater multilateral remedies.[7] It called for strengthened barriers against proliferation. All non-nuclear weapons states not party to the treaty were urged to make an internationally binding commitment to not acquire nuclear weapons and to place their nuclear programs under IAEA safeguards. All nations were urged to take safeguards into account in planning, designing, and constructing plants and fuel cycle facilities. The resolution recommended international plutonium storage as well as multinational fuel cycle facilities. It also acknowledged radiological hazards posed by attacks on nuclear plants and recommended that the Committee on Disarmament conclude its work on the matter. When discussing terrorism, the conferees encouraged adherence to the convention on the physical protection of nuclear material at the earliest date. In the realm of safety, the IAEA was asked to provide greater assistance to developing nations in siting, constructing, and operating nuclear plants. Further support for the nuclear energy regime was provided after the conference when the IAEA convened the annual meeting of its membership. In a surprise move, China announced that it would open some of its atomic plants to international inspection.[8]

All of these positive steps point toward greater application of the preventive medicine presented in this volume in the form of the proposed INRs. This is not to say that the road ahead for the INRs or like programs will be easy. Indeed, at the annual IAEA meeting some nations expressed their disgruntlement with the superpowers' manipulation of the NPT review conference.[9] More serious will be the difficulty of inducing non-NPT signatories such as Israel, India, Pakistan, Argentina, and Brazil to join the nuclear regime. Still, the 1985 review conference represented an important milestone in reinforcing the global nuclear energy regime's treatment of proliferation, terrorism, attacks on atomic plants, and accidents. The remaining work for nations interested in world safety is to build goodwill toward the regime by applying the principles of preventive medicine to ensure that nuclear energy risks are minimized.

Notes

Preface

1. Office of Technology Assessment, *Nuclear Power in an Age of Uncertainty* (Washington DC: Office of Technology Assessment, 1984), p. 3.

2. William Walker and Mans Lönnroth, "Proliferation and Nuclear Trade: A Look Ahead," *Bulletin of the Atomic Scientists* 40 (April 1984):33.

3. For elaboration of the principles of preventive medicine see Duncan W. Clark and Brian MacMahon, *Preventive Medicine* (Boston: Little, Brown and Co., 1967).

Chapter 1

1. Atomic Industrial Forum, *INFO: News Release* (Washington, DC: Atomic Industrial Forum, March 31, 1983).

2. J. J. Lave, "Nuclear Energy: Facing the Future," *International Atomic Energy Agency Bulletin* (Supplement, 1982):11.

3. Daniel S. Greenberg, "Nuclear Energy Future Slow But Sure," *Los Angeles Times* (February 19, 1984) IV:5.

4. Office of Technology Assessment, *Nuclear Power in an Age of Uncertainty* (Washington, DC: Office of Technology Assessment, 1984), pp. 179–188.

5. For an elaboration of fuel services worldwide see Congressional Research Service, *Nuclear Proliferation Factbook* (Washington, DC: Government Printing Office, 1980), pp. 173–226.

6. William Walker and Mans Lönnroth, *Nuclear Power Struggles: Industrial Competition and Proliferation Control* (London: Allen & Unwin), p. 47.

7. Ibid., p. 117.

8. Ibid., pp. 88–89; and Lewis A. Dunn, "The Emerging Nuclear Suppliers," paper presented to Georgetown University Center for International and Strategic Affairs Conference on Nuclear Suppliers and Non-Proliferation, June 28–29, 1984.

9. Walker and Lönnroth, *Nuclear Power Struggles*, p. 83.

10. Richard J. Barber Associates, *LDC Nuclear Power Prospects, 1975–1990: Commercial, Economic and Security Implications* (Springfield, VA: National Technical Information Service, n.d.), pp. IV-36, IV-38, IV-43.

11. Patrick O'Heffernan, Amory B. Lovins, and L. Hunger Lovins, *The First Nuclear World War* (New York: William Morrow & Co., 1983), p. 204.

12. Edward Wonder, "Nuclear Commerce and Nuclear Proliferation: Germany and Brazil, 1975," *Orbis* 21 (Summer 1977):293.

13. William W. Lowrance, "Nuclear Futures for Sale: Issues Raised by the West Germany–Brazilian Nuclear Agreement," in Abram Chayes and W. Bennett Lewis, eds., *International Arrangements for Nuclear Fuel Reprocessing* (Cambridge, MA: Ballinger, 1977), pp. 201–221.

14. Barber Associates, *LDC Nuclear Power Prospects*, IV-5–IV-30. For an interesting comparison of competitive advantages among exporters, see Walker and Lönnroth, *Nuclear Power Struggles*, p. 94.

15. Albert Wohlstetter, "Town and Country Planning Act 1971" (Santa Monica: California Seminar on Arms Control and Foreign Policy, 1977), pp. 23–33.

16. Thomas W. Graham, "The Economy of Nuclear Weapons in Nth Countries," in Dagobert L. Brito et al., eds., *Strategies for Managing Nuclear Proliferation: Economic and Political Issues* (Lexington, MA: Lexington Books, 1983), p. 12.

17. Pan Heuristics, *Moving Toward Life in a Nuclear Armed Crowd* (Los Angeles: Pan Heuristics, 1976), p. 30.

18. Mason Willrich and Theodore B. Taylor, *Nuclear Theft: Risks and Safeguards* (Cambridge, MA: Ballinger, 1973), pp. 5–9; Clarence D. Long, "Nuclear Proliferation: Can Congress Act in Time," *International Security* 1 (Spring 1977):60.

19. Stephen M. Meyer, *The Dynamics of Nuclear Proliferation* (Chicago: University of Chicago Press, 1984).

20. Lewis A. Dunn and William H. Overholt, "The Next Phase in Nuclear Proliferation Research," *Orbis* 20 (Summer 1976):501–507.

21. Shai Feldman, *Israeli Nuclear Deterrence: A Strategy for the 1980s* (New York: Columbia Univeristy Press, 1982); Fuad Jabber, *Israel and Nuclear Weapons* (London: Chatto and Windus, 1971), pp. 133, 146–147; Shlomo Aronson, "Israel's Nuclear Options," *ACIS Working Paper*

No. 7 (Los Angeles: Center for Arms Control and International Security, University of California, 1977); Robert W. Tucker, "Israel and the United States: From Dependence to Nuclear Weapons," *Commentary* 110 (November 1975):29–43; Steven Rosen, "Nuclearlization and Stability in the Middle East," in Onkar Marwah and Ann Schulz, eds., *Nuclear Proliferation and the Near-Nuclear Countries* (Cambridge, MA: Ballinger, 1975), pp. 175–184; Kenneth N. Waltz, "Toward Nuclear Peace," in Dagobert L. Brito, Michael D. Intriligator, and Adele E. Wick, eds., *Strategies for Managing Nuclear Proliferation: Economic and Political Issues* (Lexington, MA: Lexington Books, 1983), pp. 117–134; and Rodney Jones, ed., *Small Nuclear Forces and U.S. Security* (Lexington, MA: Lexington Books, 1983).

22. Bruce Russett in Brito, Intriligator, and Wick, eds., "Away from Nuclear Mythology," Ibid., pp. 135–144; Robert J. Pranger and Dale R. Tahtinen, *Nuclear Threat in the Middle East* (Washington, DC: American Enterprise Institute, 1975); Lewis A. Dunn, "The Dangers of Proliferation: Examining the Dissenters' Case," HI-2472-DP (Croton-on-Hudson, NY: Hudson Institute, 1976); Albert Wohlstetter, Henry Rowen, and Richard Brody, "Middle-East Instabilities and Distant Guarantors (and Disturbers) of the Peace: The Arab-Israeli Case," Preliminary Discussion Paper (Los Angeles: California Seminar on Arms Control and Foreign Policy, 1978), pp. 25–34; Pan Heuristics, *Moving Toward Life*, pp. 143–171; Albert Wohlstetter, "Spreading the Bomb Without Quite Breaking the Rules," *Foreign Policy* 25 (Winter 1975–1977):174–165; Lewis A. Dunn and Herman Kahn, "Trends in Nuclear Proliferation 1975–1995," HI•2336•RR/3 (Croton-on-Hudson, NY: Hudson Institute, 1975), pp. 114–147; William Epstein, *The Last Chance: Nuclear Proliferation and Arms Control* (New York: The Free Press, 1976), pp. 98–109.

23. Dunn and Kahn, Ibid., pp. 137–138.

24. Brian Jenkins, "Will Terrorists Go Nuclear," Discussion Paper No. 64 (Los Angeles: California Seminar on Arms Control and Foreign Policy, 1975), p. 4. See also N. Livingstone, "Megadeath: Radioactive Terrorism," in Yonah Alexander and Charles K. Ebinger, eds., *Political Terrorism and Energy: The Threat and Response* (New York: Praeger Publishers, 1982), pp. 141–180.

25. Pan Heuristics, *Moving Toward Life*, pp. 25–26; John A. Phillips, "How I Designed the A-Bomb (For My Physics Class)," *Science Digest* (January 1977):43–47.

26. Gail Bass and Brian Michael Jenkins, "A Review of Recent Trends in International Terrorism and Nuclear Incidents Abroad," N-1979-SL (Santa Monica: Rand Corp., April 1983).

27. Congress of the United States, Office of Technology Assessment, *Nuclear Proliferation and Safeguards* (New York: Praeger Publishers, 1977), p. 156.

28. Nuclear Energy Policy Study Group, *Nuclear Power Issues and Choices* (Cambridge, MA: Ballinger, 1977), p. 307.

29. Jenkins, "Will Terrorists Go Nuclear," pp. 22–23.

30. Gail Bass et al., "Motivations and Possible Actions of Potential Criminal Adversaries of U.S. Nuclear Programs," R-2554-SL (Santa Monica, CA: Rand Corp., 1980).

31. This fact is underscored by the failure of even the most comprehensive analyses of nuclear energy policy to even mention the subject. Among these analyses are the American Physical Society Study Group on Light-Water Reactor Safety, *Review of Modern Physics* (Summer 1975, Supplement No. 1); Nuclear Energy Policy Study Group, *Nuclear Power Issues and Choices* (Cambridge, MA: Ballinger, 1977); U.S. Energy Research and Development Administration, *U.S. Nuclear Power Activities*, ERDA 1524 (Springfield, VA: National Technical Information Service, 1976); and Nuclear Regulatory Commission, *Reactor Safety Study*, WASH 1400 (Springfield, VA: National Technical Information Service, 1975). The implications of nuclear weapons destruction in the United States have, however, been reviewed periodically at the Oak Ridge National Laboratory. The most recently published work is Conrad V. Chester and Rowena O. Chester, "Civil Defense Implications of the U.S. Nuclear Power Industry During a Large Nuclear War in the Year 2000," *Nuclear Technology* (December 1976):326–338. See also Steven A. Fetter and Kosta Tsipis, "Catastrophic Releases of Radioactivity," *Scientific American* 244 (April 1981):41–47; and Steve Fetter and Kosta Tsipis, "Catastrophic Nuclear Radiation Releases," Report No. 5 (Cambridge, MA: Program of Science and Technology for International Security, Massachusetts Institute of Technology, September 1980). Assessment of conventional weapons destruction will be found in Chester L. Cooper, "Nuclear Hostages," *Foreign Policy* 32 (Fall 1978):125–135; H. W. Lewis et al., *Risk Assessment Review Group Report of the U.S. Nuclear Regulatory Commission*, NUREG/CR-4000 (Washington, DC: Nuclear Regulatory Commission, 1978), p. 45; Bennett Ramberg, *Destruction of Nuclear Energy Facilities in War: The Problem and the Implications* (Lexington, MA: Lexington Books, 1980); Bennett Ramberg, "Attacks on Nuclear Reactors: The Implications of Israel's Strike on Osiraq," *Political Science Quarterly* 97 (Winter 1982–83):653–669; and Bennett Ramberg, *Nuclear Power Plants as Weapons for the Enemy: An Unrecognized Military Peril* (Berkeley: University of California Press, 1984).

32. There has been some debate over how extensive the contamination would have been had the reactor been in operation. The Congressional Research Service concluded that it would have been limited to the reactor site. The problem would not have been significant, except for pieces of the core. See House of Representatives, Committee on Foreign Relations Subcommittees on International Security and Scientific Affairs on Europe and the Middle East and on International Economic Policy and Trade, Hearings, "Israeli Attack on Iraqi Nuclear Facilities," 97th Congress, 1st Session (Washington DC: Government Printing Office, 1981), p. 156. Frank von Hipple and Jan Beyea, nuclear physicists who have written several reactor-accident-consequence studies under the auspices of Princeton University's Center for Energy and Environmental Studies, reviewed the congressional report, and concluded it was inaccurate because it analogized the effects of radium for fission products (telephone conversation with Jan Beyea, April 30, 1982). Steve Ramos, a Nuclear Regulatory Commission official who formerly directed the safety program for U.S. research reactors, contended that "significant" radioactive fallout from such facilities would not extend beyond two miles. See Eliot Marshall, "Iraqi Nuclear Program Halted by Bombing," *Science* 210 (October 31, 1980):507–508. For further elaboration of this debate, see Ramberg, *Nuclear Power Plants as Weapons*, p. xxxi, n. 10.

33. See Ramberg, *Destruction of Nuclear Energy Facilities;* "Attacks on Nuclear Reactors"; and *Nuclear Power Plants as Weapons.*

34. Royal Commission on Environmental Pollution, *Sixth Report: Nuclear Power and the Environment* (London: Her Majesty's Stationery Office, 1976), pp. 123–124.

35. See Ramberg, *Destruction of Nuclear Energy Facilities;* "Attacks on Nuclear Reactors"; and *Nuclear Power Plants as Weapons.*

36. Union of Concerned Scientists, *The Risks of Nuclear Power Plant Reactors: A Review of NRC Reactor Safety Study WASH-1400 (NUREG-75/014)* (Cambridge, MA: Union of Concerned Scientists, 1977), p. 116. The most intense examination of reactor safety is the Nuclear Regulatory Commission, *Reactor Safety Study.* A critique of the study will be found in Union of Concerned Scientists, *The Risks of Nuclear Power Plant Reactors;* American Physical Society Study Group on Light-Water Reactor Safety, *Review of Modern Physics;* Richard E. Webb, *The Accident Hazards of Nuclear Power Plants* (Amherst: The University of Massachusetts Press, 1976); and Ad Hoc Risk Assessment Review Group, *Risk Assessment Review Group Report to the U.S. Nuclear Regulatory Commission,* NUREG/CR-0400 (Washington, DC: U.S. Nuclear Regulatory Commission, 1978). For a reconsideration of the

debate see Doan L. Phung, "Technical Note: LWR Safety after TMI," *Nuclear Safety* 25 (May-June 1984):317–323 and American Physical Society, *Report to the American Physical Society of the Study Group on Radionuclide Release from Severe Accidents at Nuclear Power Plants*, draft, February 1985.

37. Zhores A. Medvedev, *Nuclear Disaster in the Urals* (New York: W. W. Norton & Co., 1979).

Chapter 2

1. Treaty on the Non-Proliferation of Nuclear Weapons, in U.S. Arms Control and Disarmament Agency, *Arms Control and Disarmament Agreements* (Washington, DC: U.S. Arms Control and Disarmament Agency, 1975), pp. 85–89.

2. Ryukichi Imai, "Nuclear Safeguards," *Adelphi Papers*, No. 86 (London: International Institute for Strategic Studies, 1972), pp. 4–6.

3. International Atomic Energy Agency, "NPT Newsletter," *International Atomic Energy Agency Bulletin* 25 (December 1983):40.

4. F. Klik, "Field Experience of Safeguards Inspectors," *International Atomic Energy Agency Bulletin* 23 (December 1981):15.

5. Comptroller General of the United States, *Role of the International Atomic Energy Agency in Safeguarding Nuclear Material* (Washington, DC: Comptroller General of the United States, 1975), pp. 24–26; and Carl Posey, "On the Uranium Trail," *Atlantic Monthly* 253 (June 1984):22–30.

6. Imai, "Nuclear Safeguards," pp. 33–34.

7. Comptroller General of the United States, *Role of the IAEA*, p. 32.

8. United States Senate, Committee on Government Operations, *Export Reorganization Act of 1976* (Hearings) (Washington, DC: Government Printing Office, 1976), pp. 963–1036.

9. *Washington Post*, October 6, 1977, p. A20.

10. Ibid.

11. Subcommittees on International Security and Scientific Affairs and International Economic Policy and Trade, Committee on Foreign Affairs, House of Representatives, 97th Congress, 2d session, March 3 and 18, 1982, *The International Atomic Energy Agency: Improving Safeguards* (Washington, DC: Government Printing Office, 1982), p. 228.

12. Committee on Foreign Relations, United States Senate, 97th Congress, 1st session, June 18, 19, and 25, 1981, *The Israeli Air Strike* (Washington, DC: Government Printing Office, 1981), p. 121.

13. Ibid., pp. 120–124.

14. Ibid., p. 123.

15. Ibid.

16. H. Gruemm, "Safeguards and Tamuz: Setting the Record Straight," *International Atomic Energy Agency Bulletin* 23 (December 1981):10–14.

17. Ibid., p. 13.

18. Comptroller General of the United States, *The Nuclear Non-Proliferation Act of 1978 Should be Selectively Modified* (Washington, DC: General Accounting Office, May 21, 1981), p. 45; Committee on Foreign Relations, Senate, *IAEA Programs of Safeguards* (Washington, DC: Government Printing Office), pp. 48, 62, 67, 79, and 80.

19. William Walker and Mans Lönnroth, *Nuclear Power Struggles: Industrial Competition and Proliferation Control* (London: Allen & Unwin), p. 122.

20. International Atomic Energy Agency, "The Physical Protection of Nuclear Material," INFCIR C/225/Rev. 1 (Vienna: International Atomic Energy Agency, 1977).

21. Convention on the Physical Protection of Nuclear Material, in Mohmad I. Shaker, ed., *The Nuclear Non-Proliferation Treaty* (London: Oceana Publications) vol. 3, pp. 1429–1439.

22. E. Iansiti, "The Development and Implications of International Safety Standards," *International Atomic Energy Agency Bulletin* 25 (September 1983):34–38.

23. Daniel Ford, *The Cult of the Atom* (New York: Simon & Shuster, 1982).

24. Subcommittee on International Economic Policy and Trade, Committee on Foreign Affairs, House of Representatives, 96th Congress, 2d Session, *Nuclear Exports: International Safety and Environmental Issues* (Washington, DC: Government Printing Office, 1980).

25. Ibid., pp. 4–5. See also "Sparks Fly Over Philippine Nuclear Plant," *The Christian Science Monitor*, November 30, 1984, p. 21.

26. Nuclear Suppliers Group, "Guidelines for Nuclear Transfers," mimeograph. See also William C. Potter, *Nuclear Power and Nonproliferation: An Interdisciplinary Perspective* (Cambridge, MA: Oelgeschlager, Gunn & Hain, 1984), pp. 44–46.

27. Stockholm International Peace Research Institute, *World Armaments and Disarmament: SIPRI Yearbook 1977* (Cambridge, MA: MIT Press, 1977), p. 22.

28. Walker and Lönnroth, *Nuclear Power Struggles*, pp. 148–152; Peter A. Clausen, "Nonproliferation Illusions: Tarapur in Retrospect,"

Orbis 27 (Fall 1983):754–756; and Warren Donnelly, private communication, July 8, 1984.

29. Walker and Lönnroth, *Nuclear Power Struggles*, pp. 148–152.

30. Ibid., p. 156.

31. Peter Clausen, "Nuclear Conference Yields Potential New Consensus," *Arms Control Today* 9 (June 1979):1–6; Stockhold International Peace Research Institute, *World Armaments and Disarmament: SIPRI Yearbook 1979* (London: Taylor and Francis, Ltd.), pp. 322–326; Congressional Research Service, *European Reactions to the International Nuclear Fuel Cycle Evaluation*, 97th Congress, 2d Session, prepared for the Subcommittee on Energy, Nuclear Proliferation, and Government Processes of the Committee on Government Affairs, U.S. Senate (Washington, DC: Government Printing Office, Aug. 1982).

32. Clausen, "Nuclear Conference Yields New Consensus," p. 4.

33. For elaboration of this discussion, see Bennett Ramberg, *Nuclear Power Plants as Weapons for the Enemy: An Unrecognized Military Peril* (Berkeley, CA: University of California Press, 1984).

34. Ibid.

35. For assessments of EURATOM, see Jaroslav G. Polach, *EURATOM: Its Background, Issues and Economic Implications* (Dobbs Ferry, NY: Oceana Publications, 1964); Henry Nau, *National Politics and International Technology* (Baltimore, MD: The Johns Hopkins University Press, 1974); Lawrence Schienman, "EURATOM: Nuclear Integration in Europe," *International Conciliation* 563 (May 1967); and Patrick O'Heffernan, Amory B. Lovins, and L. Hunter Lovins, *The First Nuclear World War* (New York: William Morrow & Co., 1983), pp. 239–240.

36. Treaty Establishing the European Atomic Energy Community, Article 77.

37. European Committee Information Service, *Press Release*, No. 5/1977 (February 18, 1977); Protocol to the IAEA/EURATOM Safeguards Agreement.

38. Treaty Establishing the European Atomic Energy Community, Article 81.

39. Ibid., Article 83.

40. The treaty will be found in United States Arms Control and Disarmament Agency, *Arms Control and Disarmament Agreements* (Washington, DC: United States Arms Control and Disarmament Agency, 1962), pp. 59–81; for an analysis of the treaty see William Epstein, *The Last Chance: Nuclear Proliferation and Arms Control* (New York: The Free Press, 1976), pp. 211–214.

41. United States Arms Control and Disarmament Agency, Article 16.

42. Stockholm International Peace Research Institute, *SIPRI Yearbook 1981* (Cambridge, MA: Oelgeschlager, Gunn & Hain, 1981), pp. 418–434.

43. Gloria Duffy, "Soviet Nuclear Exports," *International Security* 3 (Summer 1978):87.

44. Comptroller General of the United States, *Overview of Nuclear Export Policies of Major Foreign Supplier Nations* (Washington, DC: General Accounting Office, 1977); United States Congress, "Nuclear Non-Proliferation Act of 1978," Public Law 95-242, March 10, 1978.

45. Congress of the United States, Office of Technology Assessment, *Nuclear Proliferation and Safeguards* (New York: Praeger Publishers, 1977), p. 218.

46. According to a U.S. General Accounting Office report, in the 1970s security at an Italian nuclear storage facility (presumably under EURATOM safeguard) was "very lax." Doors to storage areas containing highly enriched uranium were found ajar. At one facility, radioactive material was found next to an open window. At another, chicken wire cages protected bomb-grade products. John Fialka, "Transporting Atomic Materials Poses a Major Problem," in House of Representatives, Committee on International Relations, Subcommittee on International Security and Scientific Affairs, 95th Congress, 1st Session, *The Nuclear Antiproliferation Act of 1977* (Washington, DC: Government Printing Office, 1977), p. 336.

47. Benjamin N. Schiff, *International Nuclear Technology Transfer: Dilemmas of Dissemination and Control* (Totowa, NJ: Rowman & Allanheld), p. 36.

48. Ibid., pp. 36–37.

49. Statement by Bernard Baruch, U.S. Representative to the United Nations Atomic Energy Commission, June 14, 1946, in *Documents on Disarmament 1945–1959*, vol. 1, U.S. Arms Control and Disarmament Agency, pp. 7–11.

50. Johns W. Spanier and Joseph L. Nogee, *The Politics of Disarmament: A Study in Soviet-American Gamesmanship* (New York: Praeger Publishers, 1962), pp. 56–75.

51. Schiff, *International Nuclear Technology Transfer*, pp. 45–49.

52. Ibid., pp. 48–55.

53. Pierre Lellouche, *Internationalization of the Nuclear Fuel Cycle and Non-Proliferation Strategy: Lessons and Prospects* (Cambridge, MA: Harvard Law School, SJD dissertation, 1979), p. 161.

54. Ibid., p. 162.

55. Robert Pendley and Lawrence Schienman, "International Safeguarding Institutionalized Collective Behavior," *International Organization* 29 (Summer 1974):585–616.

56. Lellouche, *Nuclear Fuel Cycle*, pp. 163–64.

57. William C. Potter, "Managing Proliferation: Problems and Prospects for U.S.-Soviet Cooperation," in Dagobert L. Brito, Michael D. Intriligator, and Adele E. Wick, eds., *Strategies for Managing Nuclear Proliferation* (Lexington, MA: Lexington Books, 1983), p. 248.

58. Schiff, *International Nuclear Technology Transfer*, pp. 99–106.

59. Back issues of the *International Atomic Energy Agency Bulletin*, which catalogues these endeavors, and IAEA press release PR 84/14, June 8, 1984.

60. Stockholm International Peace Research Institute, *SIPRI Yearbook 1983* (New York: Taylor and Francis, 1983), p. 72.

61. Subcommittees on International Security and Scientific Affairs, *The International Atomic Energy Agency*, p. 64.

62. Askoh Kapur, "Proliferation Prospects in Secondary Conflict Zones," paper presented to the 24th Annual Convention of the International Studies Convention, Mexico City, April 1983.

63. P. R. Johannson, "Canada and the Quest for International Nuclear Security," in Robert Boardman and James F. Keeley, eds., *Nuclear Exports and World Politics: Policy and Regime* (New York: St. Martin's Press, 1983), pp. 79–97.

64. Steve Weissman and Herbert Krosney, *The Islamic Bomb* (New York: Times Books, 1981), pp. 151–152; and Michael J. Brenner, *Nuclear Power and Non-Proliferation: The Remaking of U.S. Policy* (Cambridge, England: Cambridge University Press, 1982), p. 118.

65. Pierre Lellouche, "The Dilemmas of Non-proliferation Policy: The Supplier Countries," in David Carlton and Carlo Schaerf, eds., *The Arms Race in the 1980s* (New York: St. Martin's Press, 1982), pp. 180–181.

66. Richard K. Betts, "A Diplomatic Bomb? South Africa's Nuclear Potential," in Joseph Yager, ed., *Nonproliferation and U.S. Foreign Policy* (Washington, DC: Brookings Institution, 1980), pp. 300–301.

67. Stockholm International Peace Research Institute, *SIPRI Yearbook 1976* (Cambridge, MA: MIT Press, 1967), pp. 6–11.

68. Stockholm International Peace Research Institute, *SIPRI Yearbook 1981* (Cambridge, MA: Oelgeschlager, Gunn & Hain, 1981), pp. 297–372.

69. Iansiti, "Development and Implications."

70. Charles N. Van Doren, *Nuclear Supply and Non-Proliferation: The IAEA Committee on Assurances of Supply*, Report No. 83-202 S (Washington, DC: Congressional Research Service, 1983).

71. International Atomic Energy Agency, *International Atomic Energy Agency Bulletin* 25 (December 1983), p. 40.

72. Schiff, *International Nuclear Technology Transfer*, pp. 139–141.

73. Convention on the Physical Protection of Nuclear Material, *The Nuclear Non-Proliferation Treaty*.

74. L. G. Epel et al., "IAEA Efforts to Improve Nuclear Power Plant Operational Safety," *International Atomic Energy Agency Bulletin* 25 (September 1983):8.

75. "IAEA Conference Concentrates on Israel, South Africa," *Nuclear Engineering International* 29 (November 1984):6.

76. Stockholm International Peace Research Institute, *SIPRI Yearbook 1983*, p. 78.

Chapter 3

1. Section 123, Atomic Energy Act of 1954 as Amended in Congressional Research Service, *Nuclear Proliferation Factbook* (Washington, DC: Government Printing Office, 1977), pp. 34–35.

2. Energy Research and Development Administration, *Final Environmental Statement: U.S. Nuclear Power Export Activities*, vol. 1 (Springfield, VA: National Technical Information Service, 1976), pp. 1–14.

3. United States Senate, Committee on Government Operations, *Export Reorganization Act of 1976*, 94th Congress, 2d Session (Washington, DC: Government Printing Office, 1976), p. 885.

4. Ibid., pp. 886–887.

5. Ibid., p. 886.

6. Energy Research and Development Administration, *Final Environmental Statement*, pp. i, 1-1.

7. Ibid., p. i.

8. Ibid., pp. 1–21.

9. Ibid., section 5-8.

10. Ibid., p. iii.

11. Ibid., pp. 14–12.

12. Nuclear Non-Proliferation Act of 1978, Public Law 95-242, March 10, 1978.

13. Horst Mendershausen, "International Cooperation in Nuclear Fuel Services; European and American Approaches," P-6308 (Santa Monica, CA: The Rand Corp., 1978), p. 5.

14. Thomas L. Neff and Henry D. Jacoby, "Nonproliferation Strategy in a Changing Nuclear Fuel Market," *Foreign Affairs* 57 (Summer 1979):1123–1143.

15. Comptroller General, *U.S. Nuclear Non-Proliferation Policy: Impact on Exports and Nuclear Industry Could Not Be Determined* (Washington, DC: General Accounting Office, 1980); Comptroller General, *The Nuclear Non-Proliferation Act of 1978 Should Be Selectively Modified* (Washington, DC: General Accounting Office, 1981), p. 120.

16. Subcommittee on International Organization and Movements and on the Near East and South Asia, Committee on Foreign Affairs, House of Representatives, *U.S. Foreign Policy and the Export of Nuclear Technology to the Middle East*, 93rd Congress, 2d Session (Washington, DC: Government Printing Office, 1974), p. 93.

17. Ibid.

18. Ibid., pp. 188, 198.

19. Ibid., pp. 100–101.

20. Congressional Research Service, *Analysis of Arms Control Impact Statements Submitted in Connection with the Fiscal Year 1976 Budget Request* (Washington, DC: Government Printing Office, 1977), pp. 350–351.

21. Ibid.

22. Ibid., pp. 4–5.

23. Ibid., pp. 6–7.

24. Ibid., pp. 8–11.

25. Robert C. Gray, "The Coordination of Arms Control Policy and the Weapons Acquisition Process: The Case of Arms Control Impact Statements," *Arms Control* 2 (Sept. 1981):218–236.

26. Treaty Establishing the European Atomic Energy Community.

27. Telephone interview with the staff of the European Information Center, Washington, DC, 1977; see also Patrick O'Heffernan, Amory B. Lovins, and L. Hunter Lovins, *The First Nuclear World War* (New York: Times Books, 1983), pp. 239–240.

28. For a review of Cocom's development see Gunnar Adler-Karlsson, *Western Economic Warfare 1947–1967* (Stockholm: Almquist and Wiksell, 1978); and Robert E. Klitgaard, *National Security and Export Controls*, R-1432-1-ARPA/CIEP (Santa Monica, CA: The Rand Corp., 1974).

29. Adler-Karlsson, *Western Economic Warfare*, pp. 52, 95.

30. Ibid., pp. 187–200; Klitgaard, *National Security*, p. 71.

31. John A. King, Jr., *Economic Development Projects and Their Appraisal* (Baltimore, MD: The Johns Hopkins Press, 1967), p. 5.

32. Ibid., pp. 3–15.

33. Edward S. Mason and Robert E. Asher, *The World Bank Since Bretton Woods* (Washington, DC: The Brookings Institution, 1973), pp. 257–259.

34. Wojciech Morawiecki, "The IAEA's Role in Promoting Physical Protection of Nuclear Material and Facilities," *International Atomic Energy Agency Bulletin* 20 (June 1978):39–45.

35. Ibid.; and Convention on the Physical Protection of Nuclear Material, in Mohamed I. Shaker, ed., *The Nuclear Non-Proliferation Treaty* (London: Oceana Publications, 1980), Vol. 3, pp. 1429–1439.

36. Oran R. Young, *Compliance and Public Authority: A Theory with International Implications* (Baltimore, MD: The Johns Hopkins University Press, 1979), p. 5.

37. I. William Zartman and Maureen R. Berman, *The Practical Negotiator* (New Haven, CT: Yale University Press, 1982), p. 72.

38. Peter A. Clausen, "Nonproliferation Illusions: Tarapur in Retrospect," *Orbis* 27 (Fall 1983):741–759.

39. Richard B. Bilder, *Managing the Risks of International Agreement* (Madison, WI: University of Wisconsin Press, 1981), p. 174.

40. Young, *Compliance and Public Authority*, pp. 67–96.

41. Arthur A. Stein, "Coordination and Collaboration: Regimes in an Anarchic World," *International Organization* 36 (Spring 1982):312–313.

42. David M. Leive, *International Regulatory Regimes* (Lexington, MA: Lexington Books), p. 584.

43. *Arms Control Today* 14 (March-April 1984).

Chapter 4

1. Stockholm International Peace Research Institute, *SIPRI Yearbook 1983* (London: Taylor & Francis, 1983), p. 96.

2. Stockholm International Peace Research Institute, *Internationalization to Prevent the Spread of Nuclear Weapons* (London: Taylor & Francis, 1980).

3. Michael J. Brenner, "Renewing the Non-Proliferation Regime: A Multilateral Approach," in Edward C. Luck, ed., *Arms Control: The Multilateral Alternative* (New York: New York University Press, 1983), p. 170.

4. Joseph A. Yager, *International Cooperation in Nuclear Energy* (Washington, DC: The Brookings Institution, 1981), p. 140.

5. Ibid., p. 142.

6. Pierre Lellouche, *Internationalization of the Nuclear Fuel Cycle and Non-Proliferation Strategy: Lessons and Prospects* (Cambridge, MA: Harvard Law School, SJD dissertation, 1979), p. 221.

7. George Quester, "Peaceful P.A.L.," *ACIS Working Paper No. 9* (Los Angeles: Center for Arms Control and International Security, University of California, 1977).

8. International Atomic Energy Agency, "The Physical Protection of Nuclear Material," INFCIRC/225/Rev.1 (Vienna: International Atomic Energy Agency, 1977), Preface.

9. Eliot Marshall, "Ultrasafe Reactors, Anyone?" *Science* 219 (January 21, 1983):265–267.

10. Lewis A. Dunn, "The Emerging Nuclear Suppliers," paper presented to Georgetown University Center for International and Strategic Affairs Conference on Nuclear Suppliers and Nuclear Non-Proliferation, June 28–29, 1984, p. 14.

11. Abraham Ribicoff, "A Market Sharing Approach to the World Nuclear Sales Problem," *Foreign Affairs* 54 (July 1976):77.

Chapter 5

1. Reviews of these options will be found in Stockholm International Peace Research Institute, *Internationalization to Prevent the Spread of Nuclear Weapons* (London: Taylor & Francis, 1980); Robert Harkavy, "International Arms Trade: The Problem of Controlling Conventional War," in William W. Whitson, ed., *Foreign Policy and U.S. National Security* (New York: Praeger, 1976); Lewis A. Dunn, "Some Reflections on the 'Dove's Dilemma,'" *International Organization* 35 (Winter 1981):181–192; George H. Quester, "Preventing Proliferation: The Impact on International Politics," *International Organization* 35 (Winter 1981):213–240; Richard Betts, "Paranoids, Pygmies, Pariahs and Non-Proliferation," *Foreign Policy* 26 (Spring 1977):157–183; and William C. Potter, *Nuclear Power and Nonproliferation: An Interdisciplinary Perspective* (Cambridge, MA: Oelgeschlager, Gunn & Hain, 1982), pp. 197–241.

2. Bennett Ramberg, *Destruction of Nuclear Energy Facilities in War: The Problem and the Implications* (Lexington, MA: Lexington Books, 1980), pp. 114–131.

3. United States Senate, Committee on Government Operations, *Export Reorganization Act of 1976*, 94th Congress, 2d session (Washington, DC: Government Printing Office, 1976), pp. 9–11.

4. Carl von Clausewitz, *On War* (Princeton, NJ: Princeton University Press, 1976).

5. Albert Wohlstetter, "Town and Country Planning Act 1971" (Santa Monica, CA: California Seminar on Arms Control and Foreign Policy, 1977).

6. Ibid., pp. 30–31.

7. Ibid., pp. 35–36.

8. Ibid.

9. Stephen M. Meyer, *The Dynamics of Nuclear Proliferation* (Chicago: University of Chicago Press, 1984).

10. William Walker and Mans Lönnroth, *Nuclear Power Struggles: Industrial Competition and Proliferation Control* (London: Allen & Unwin, 1983), p. 92.

11. Morris Rosen, "Establishment of an International Nuclear Safety Body," *International Atomic Energy Agency Bulletin* 25 (September 1983):3.

12. Committee on Foreign Relations, U.S. Senate, 97th Congress, 1st Session, December 2, 1981 (Washington, DC: Government Printing Office, 1982), p. 40.

13. Carlton R. Stoiber, "Multilateral Nuclear Supply Arrangements as a Proliferation Barrier," paper presented to Georgetown University Center for International and Strategic Affairs Conference on Nuclear Suppliers and Non-Proliferation, June 28–29, 1984, p. 17.

14. Lewis A. Dunn, "The Emerging Nuclear Suppliers," paper presented to Georgetown University Center for International and Strategic Affairs Conference on Nuclear Suppliers and Non-Proliferation, June 28–29, 1984, p. 19.

Epilogue

1. William Epstein, "A Critical Time for Nuclear Nonproliferation," *Scientific American* 253 (August 1985):33–39; Paul Leventhal, "Flaws in the Non-Proliferation Treaty," *Bulletin of the Atomic Scientists* 41 (September 1985):12–15.

2. Epstein, Ibid., 37.

3. Ibid., 39.

4. Leventhal, "Flaws in the Non-Proliferation Treaty," 14.

5. Department of State, "NPT Review Conference: Text of Final Declaration," mimeo., 1985.

6. *New York Times*, September 22, 1985, p. 12.

7. Ibid.; telephone interviews during the week of 6 October 1985 with Jackson Davis, delegate from the Pacific island nation of Nauru; Joseph Pilat, delegate from the United States; and, Warren Donnelly of the Congressional Research Service.

8. *New York Times*, September 25, 1985, p. 4.

9. Pilat interview.

Abbreviations and Acronyms

ACDA	Arms Control and Disarmament Agency
CAS	Committee on Assurances of Supply
CRS	Congressional Research Service
Cocom	Consultative Committee
EAEC; EURATOM	European Atomic Energy Community
ERDA	Energy Research and Development Administration
Eurodif	European uranium enrichment consortium
GAO	General Accounting Office
gwe	gigawatts electrical
IAEA	International Atomic Energy Agency
INFCE	International Nuclear Fuel Cycle Evaluation
INR	International Nuclear Review
INRB	International Nuclear Review Board
MUF	material unaccounted for
Mwth	megawatts thermal
Mwe	megawatts electrical
NERB	Nuclear Exporters Review Board
NNPA	Nuclear Non-Proliferation Act (1978)
NPT	Non-Proliferation Treaty
NRC	Nuclear Regulatory Commission
OSART	Operational Safety Review Team
PALs	permissive action links
SIPRI	Stockholm International Peace Research Institute

CISA Book Series: Studies in International and Strategic Affairs

The CISA Book Series, "Studies in International and Strategic Affairs," has the goal of making an original and influential contribution to the evolving literature on arms control and national security policy. Volumes in the series serve as major reference works in the field of strategic affairs. They include both innovative conceptual and historical analyses and proceedings of CISA-sponsored conferences. The CISA Book Series is edited by William C. Potter, Executive Director of CISA. Orders for these books should be placed directly with the respective publishers.

CISA Book Series

William C. Potter, Editor, *Verification and SALT: The Challenge of Strategic Deception,* Boulder, Colorado: Westview Press, 1980.

Bennett Ramberg, *Destruction of Nuclear Energy Facilities in War: The Problem and the Implications,* Lexington, Massachusetts: Lexington Books, 1980.

Paul Jabber, *Not by War Alone: Security and Arms Control in the Middle East,* Berkeley and Los Angeles: University of California Press, 1981.

Roman Kolkowicz and Andrzej Korbonski, Editors, *Soldiers, Peasants, and Bureaucrats: Civil-Military Relations in Communist and Modernizing Societies,* London and Boston: Allen & Unwin, 1982.

William C. Potter, *Nuclear Power and Nonproliferation: An Interdisciplinary Perspective,* Cambridge, Massachusetts: Oelgeschlager, Gunn & Hain, 1982.

Steven L. Spiegel, Editor, *The Middle East and the Western Alliance,* London and Boston: Allen & Unwin, 1982.

Bennett Ramberg, *Zielscheibe Kernkraftwerk: Kernkraftwerke im Kriegsfall,* Munich, Federal Republic of Germany: Karamanolis-Verlag, 1982.

Dagobert L. Brito, Michael D. Intriligator, and Adele E. Wick, Editors, *Strategies for Managing Nuclear Proliferation: Economic and Political Issues,* Lexington, Massachusetts: Lexington Books, 1983.

Bernard Brodie, Michael D. Intriligator, and Roman Kolkowicz, Editors, *National Security and International Stability,* Cambridge, Massachusetts: Oelgeschlager, Gunn & Hain, 1983.

Raju G. C. Thomas, Editor, *The Great Power Triangle and Asian Security,* Lexington, Massachusetts: Lexington Books, 1983.

R. D. Tschirgi, *The Politics of Indecision: Origins and Implications of American Involvement with the Palestine Problem,* New York: Praeger, 1983.

G. Luciani, Editor, *The Mediterranean Region: Economic Interdependence and the Future of Society,* New York: St. Martin's Press, and London: Croom Helm, 1984.

Roman Kolkowicz and Neil Joeck, Editors, *Arms Control and International Security,* Boulder, Colorado: Westview Press, 1984.

Jiri Valenta and William C. Potter, Editors, *Soviet Decisionmaking for National Security,* London and Boston: Allen & Unwin, 1984.

Raju G. C. Thomas, *Indian Security Policy,* Princeton: Princeton University Press, forthcoming.

Bennett Ramberg, *Nuclear Power Plants as Weapons for the Enemy: An Unrecognized Military Peril*, Berkeley and Los Angeles: University of California Press, 1984.

William C. Potter, Editor, *Verification and Arms Control*, Lexington, Massachusetts: Lexington Books, 1985.

Rodney Jones, Cesare Merlini, Joseph Pilat and William C. Potter, Editors, *The Nuclear Suppliers and Nonproliferation: International Policy Choices*, Lexington, Massachusetts: Lexington Books, 1985.

Bennett Ramberg, *Global Nuclear Energy Risks: The Search for Preventive Medicine*, Boulder, Colorado: Westview Press, 1985.

Index

ACDA. *See* Arms Control and
Disarmament Agency
Agency for the Prohibition of
Nuclear Weapons in Latin
America, 38–39
Argentina
adherence to the Treaty for the
Prohibition of Nuclear
Weapons in Latin America,
39
nuclear exports, 71, 83
nuclear generation, 1, 3
nuclear imports, 7, 35
and nuclear war, 13, 14
nuclear weapons and disputes,
14
nuclear weapons capability, 24
plutonium in spent fuel in, 11
Arms Control and Disarmament
Agency (U.S.), 49, 50, 64, 65,
84
arms control assessments, 56–58
nuclear export review, 55–56
Atomic Energy Act (U.S.), 50
Atoms for Peace Plan, 41
Australia
nuclear export controls, 39
nuclear generation, 5
plutonium in spent fuel in, 10
Austria, 1, 2, 3
plutonium in spent fuel in, 10

Bangladesh
plutonium in spent fuel in, 11
Baruch Plan, 40
Belgium
Cocom membership, 58
EURODIF membership, 6

nuclear fabrication, 6
nuclear generation, 1, 2, 3
nuclear imports, 94
plutonium in spent fuel in, 10
reprocessing in, 6
Berman, Maureen R., 62
Bilder, Richard, 63
Brazil
adherence to the Treaty for the
Prohibition of Nuclear
Weapons in Latin America,
39
nuclear exports, 7, 83
nuclear generation, 2, 3
nuclear imports, 8
and nuclear war, 13, 14
nuclear weapons and disputes,
14
nuclear weapons capability, 24
plutonium in spent fuel in, 11
Brenner, Michael, 67, 69
Britain
Cocom membership, 58
nuclear export controls, 39
nuclear fabrication, 6
nuclear generation, 1, 2, 3, 5
nuclear imports, 94
and nuclear war, 13
nuclear weapons and disputes,
14
as a nuclear weapons state, 9,
41
plutonium in spent fuel in, 10
URENCO membership, 6
Bulgaria
nuclear generation, 2, 3

123